A MANGA LOVER'S TOKYO TRAVEL GUIDE

T0047117

TUTTLE Publishing

Tokyo | Rutland, Vermont | Singapore

CONTENTS

WHAT TO BRING ALONG 4

INTRODUCTION 5

GETTING AROUND 6
SURVIVAL JAPANESE 8

CHAPTER 1
EXPLORING TRADITIONAL TOKYO 10

THE IMPERIAL PALACE GARDENS 12
VISITING THE MEIJI SHRINE IN HARAJUKU 14
A VISIT TO ASAKUSA 18
A KIMONO MAKEOVER IN ASAKUSA 22
A STROLL AROUND UENO 27
VISITING A HOT SPRING BATH IN ODAIBA 31
GARDENS AND NATURE WALKS 36
VISITING MT. FUJI 38

CHAPTER 2
ANIMANGA TOKYO 46

OTAKU PARADISE AKIHABARA 48
VISITING AN AKIBA MAID CAFE 52
AN IKEBUKURO BUTLER CAFE 58
AT A COSPLAY STUDIO 64
TOKYO ONE PIECE TOWER 68
THE GUNDAM STATUE IN ODAIBA 72
NAKANO BROADWAY 74
TAKING A MANGA CLASS IN NAKANO 76
THE GHIBLI MUSEUM 78
SANRIO PUROLAND 82
THE DORAEMON MUSEUM 86

CHAPTER 3

ADVENTURES IN JAPANESE FOOD 90

JAPANESE NOODLES 92
SUSHI 95
YAKITORI 99
SUKIYAKI AND SHABU-SHABU 100
OTHER JAPANESE DISHES 101
EATING ON A BUDGET 103
TRADITIONAL JAPANESE DESSERT 105
JAPANESE DRINKS 106

CHAPTER 4

SHOPPING HEAVEN 108

TAX-FREE SHOPPING 109
SHOPPING FOR SOUVENIRS 110
THE UBIQUITOUS 100 YEN SHOPS 113
AWESOME ELECTRONICS 114
COSMETICS AND BEAUTY PRODUCTS 115
CONVENIENCE STORES 116
TOKYO'S MAIN SHOPPING DISTRICTS 119
BUYING KAWAII CLOTHES 120
BOOKS AND MAGAZINES 123
ART MATERIALS 125

WHAT TO BRING ALONG

INTRODUCTION

GETTING AROUND

ONCE YOU GET TO TOKYO, PUBLIC TRANSPORT IS VERY CONVENIENT:

CAB

CABS ARE ALMOST EVERYWHERE BUT VERY EXPENSIVE. TAKING A CAB FROM ONE TRAIN STATION TO THE NEXT WILL COST AROUND 1,000 YEN.

BUS

WAITING TIMES VARY BUT ARE USUALLY QUITE LONG. CENTRAL TOKYO BUSES CHARGE A FLAT FARE OF 210 YEN THAT YOU PAY WHEN YOU GET ON.

TRAIN/SUBWAY

THERE ARE MANY DIFFERENT TRAIN AND SUBWAY LINES, AND IT'S EASY TO TRANSFER BETWEEN THEM. TOILETS ARE ALWAYS AVAILABLE INSIDE THE STATIONS AFTER THE TICKET GATES.

YOU CAN BUY CHARGE CARDS FROM VENDING MACHINES AT STATIONS. PASMO AND SUICA CARDS CAN BE USED FOR ANY BUS OR TRAIN.

THE MINIMUM CHARGE IS 1,000 YEN FOR A PASMO CARD AND 2,000 YEN FOR A SUICA. GET LEFTOVER MONEY REFUNDED AT THE STATION OFFICE BEFORE YOU LEAVE JAPAN.

THE MOST SIGNIFICANT TRAIN LINE IN TOKYO IS THE YAMANOTE LINE, AKA THE GREEN LINE.

SOME EXPRESS TRAINS SKIP STOPS FOR A SHORTER TRAVELING TIME.

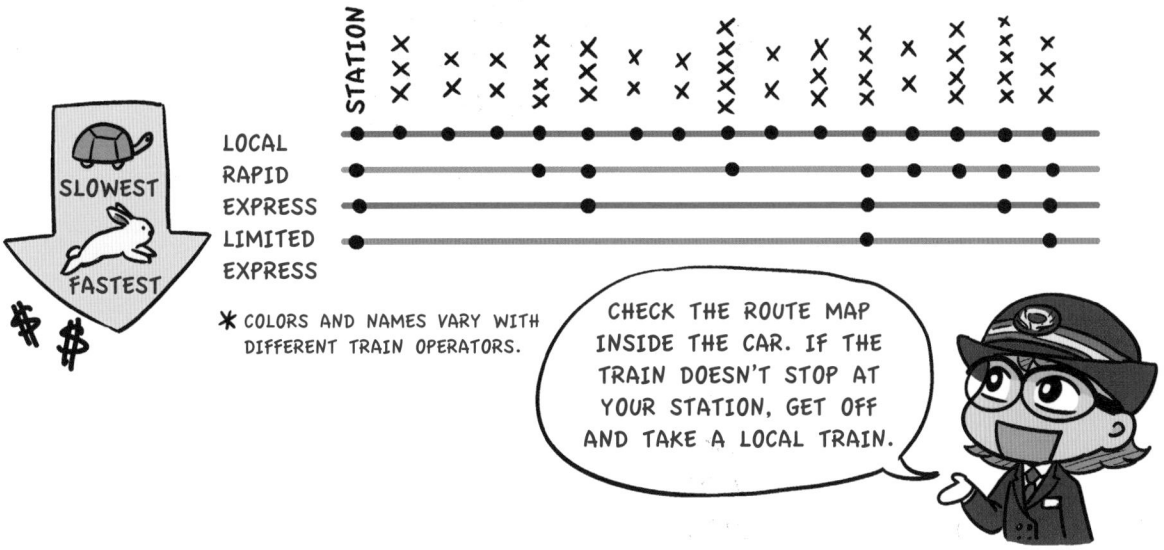

* COLORS AND NAMES VARY WITH DIFFERENT TRAIN OPERATORS.

IF YOU ARE TRAVELING TO OTHER PREFECTURES, YOU CAN BUY A JR PASS IN YOUR HOME COUNTRY FOR THE SHINKANSEN, THE FAMOUS BULLET TRAIN. PLANS ARE AVAILABLE HERE: www.jreast.co.jp/e/

SURVIVAL JAPANESE

ENGLISH IS WIDELY UNDERSTOOD IN TOKYO NOW BUT IT HELPS TO LEARN A FEW BASIC WORDS OF JAPANESE. HERE ARE SOME VERY USEFUL ONES.

GREETINGS

OHAYO GOZAIMASU
GOOD MORNING

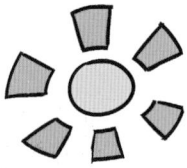

KONNICHIWA
GOOD AFTERNOON

KONBANWA
GOOD EVENING

OYASUMI
GOOD NIGHT

ARIGATO GOZAIMASU
THANK YOU

SUMIMASEN
EXCUSE ME/SORRY

NUMBERS

1	ichi	**6**	roku	**11**	juu-ichi	**hitotsu**	one thing or object
2	ni	**7**	shichi/nana	**12**	juu-ni, etc	**futatsu**	two things or objects
3	san	**8**	hachi	**100**	hyaku	**mittsu**	three things or objects
4	shi/yon	**9**	kyuu	**1,000**	sen	**yottsu**	four things or objects
5	go	**10**	juu	**10,000**	ichiman	**itsutsu**	five things or objects

EXPRESSIONS

HOW MUCH IS IT? → IKURA DESUKA?

I DON'T UNDERSTAND. → WAKARIMASEN.

CAN YOU PLEASE REPEAT? → MO ICHIDO KUDASAI.

I'LL TAKE (BUY) THAT ONE. → KORE KUDASAI.

PLEASE → ONEGAI SHIMASU.

HOW DO I GET THERE? → DOYATTE IKIMASUKA?

DIRECTIONS

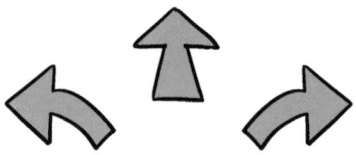

HIDARI
LEFT

MIGI
RIGHT

MASSUGU
STRAIGHT AHEAD

GETTING AROUND

THE JAPANESE ARE VERY HELPFUL, SO JUST SAYING YOU ARE GOING TO A PLACE WITH A PUZZLED OR WORRIED TONE IS UNDERSTOOD AS ASKING FOR DIRECTIONS.

EXCUSE ME, I WANT TO GO TO _____.
(PLACE)

OR

EXCUSE ME, WHERE IS _____?
(PLACE)

EATING OUT

① THE WAITER WILL ASK HOW MANY PEOPLE YOU HAVE.

* "NAN-MEI SAMA" IS A POLITE FORM OF ASKING "HOW MANY OF YOU?"

② REPLY WITH THE NUMBER OF PEOPLE.

③ THE WAITER WILL TAKE ORDER FOR DRINKS FIRST.

④ AFTER YOU HAVE EATEN, ASK FOR THE BILL.

⑤ THANK THE CASHIER WHEN LEAVING.

CHAPTER 1

EXPLORING TRADITIONAL TOKYO

JAPAN IS A COUNTRY THAT MAKES A GREAT EFFORT TO PRESERVE ITS CULTURAL HERITAGE AND HISTORY.
FROM THE KIMONO TO THE TEA CEREMONY AND SUMO WRESTLING, THE JAPANESE PLACE A LOT OF EMPHASIS ON MAINTAINING THE TRADITIONS PASSED DOWN THROUGH THE GENERATIONS.
IN THIS CHAPTER, I WILL TAKE YOU TO SOME HISTORICAL PLACES, INTRODUCE YOU TO KIMONO AND YUKATA...
...SHOW YOU HOW TO TAKE A HOT SPRING BATH...
...AND THE PROPER WAY TO PRAY AT TEMPLES AND SHRINES.

THE IMPERIAL PALACE GARDENS

THE GARDENS ARE AN EASY 15 MINUTE WALK FROM THE MARUNOUCHI CENTRAL EXIT OF TOKYO STATION AND JUST A 5 MINUTE WALK FROM EXIT D2 OF OTEMACHI STATION.

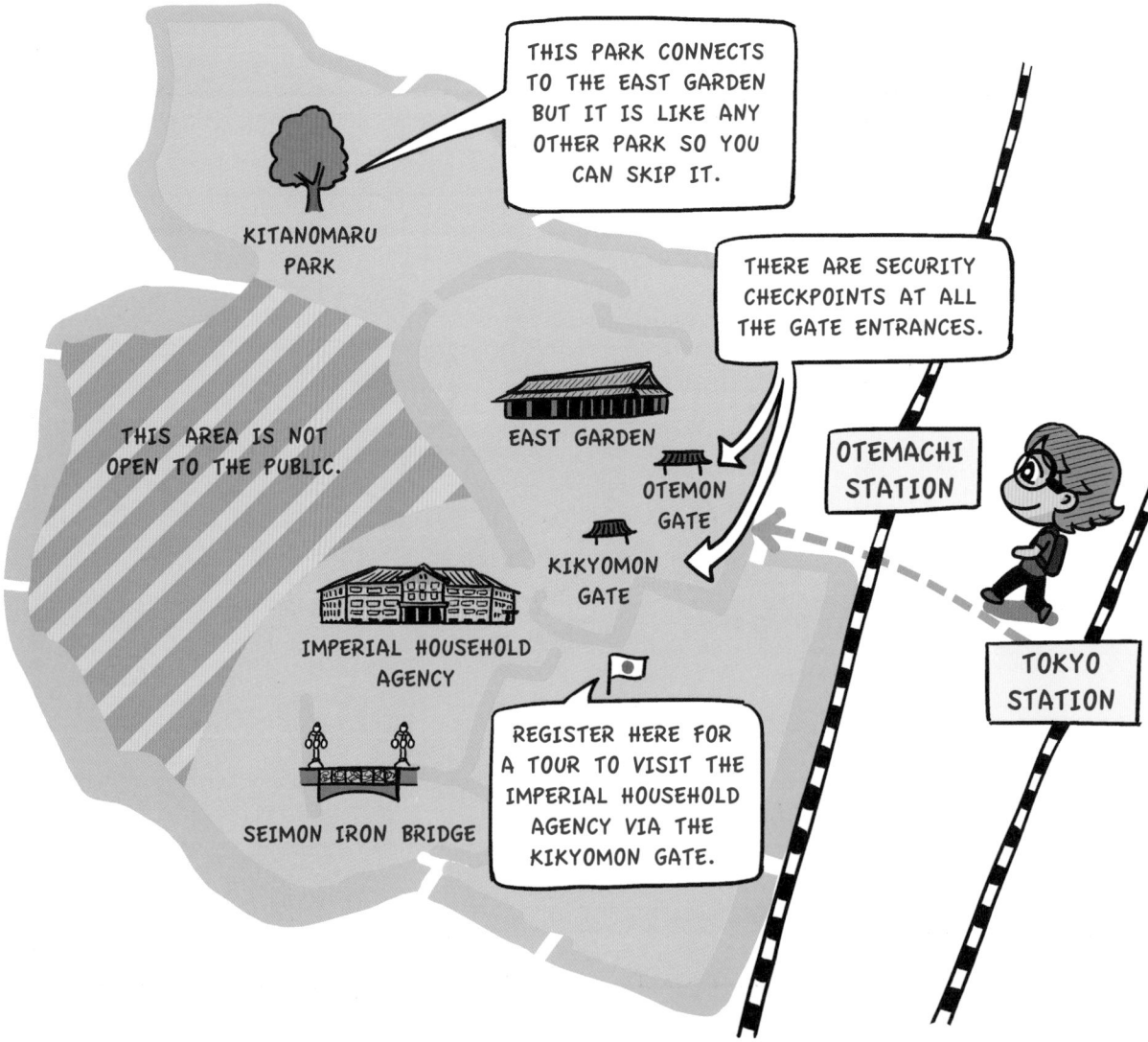

THERE ARE 2 GUIDED TOURS A DAY AT 10AM AND 1.30PM AND YOU CAN REGISTER ON THE DAY ITSELF AT THE KIKYOMON GATE.
YOU'LL NEED YOUR PASSPORT OR ID IN ORDER TO BE GIVEN A PASS.
145

THE TOUR HAS A LOT OF WALKING AND LASTS FOR AROUND 75 MIN.
BUT EVERYTHING IS IN JAPANESE SO YOU MAY WANT TO DOWNLOAD THE IMPERIAL PALACE APP FOR THE AUDIO TRANSLATION.
BLA BLA
BLA BLA

THE COOL PART OF THE TOUR IS STANDING ON THE ICONIC IRON BRIDGE THAT ALWAYS APPEARS IN PHOTOS BUT ISN'T OPEN TO THE PUBLIC UNLESS YOU ARE ON THIS TOUR.

BUT EVEN IF YOU DON'T TAKE THE TOUR, THE EAST GARDEN IS REALLY NICE TO VISIT ANYWAY.
THERE ARE SOME OLD BUILDINGS HERE, SUCH AS THIS GUARDHOUSE.

THOUGH FOR SOME SITES, LIKE THE PINE-TREE CORRIDOR CALLED "MATSU-NO-ROKA" THERE'S NOTHING LEFT BUT A SIGNBOARD.
THAT'S IT?
松之大廊下跡

VISITING THE GARDENS WAS A MIXTURE OF EXERCISE AND DISCOVERY FOR ME SO I HOPE YOU WILL ENJOY YOUR VISIT TOO!

VISITING THE MEIJI SHRINE IN HARAJUKU

MEIJI SHRINE IS CALLED "MEIJI JINGU" IN JAPANESE AND IS LOCATED INSIDE A LARGE PARK. THERE ARE 2 ENTRANCES—THE ONE AT HARAJUKU STATION IS THE MORE POPULAR ONE.

KITASANDO STATION

MEIJI SHRINE

YOU HAVE TO WALK 700M FROM HERE.

HARAJUKU STATION

SHIBUYA STATION

FOREIGNERS SOMETIMES GET CONFUSED ABOUT THE DIFFERENCE BETWEEN A SHRINE AND A BUDDHIST TEMPLE.

"JINJA"= SHRINE FOR LOCAL GODS

"OTERA"=TEMPLE FOR BUDDHA OR A BODDHISATVA LIKE THE GODDESS OF MERCY

THE PATH WAS ALSO GRAVELED SO IT MADE PUSHING THE STROLLER NEARLY IMPOSSIBLE...
WE NEED TO TAKE A BREAK.
GOSH! PEOPLE IN WHEELCHAIRS WILL HAVE PROBLEMS TOO!

LUCKILY THERE WAS A RESTAURANT NEARBY SO WE COULD REST A WHILE.
HEY, THERE'S A GARDEN HERE?
YES... BUT YOU'LL NEED TO PAY TO ENTER...

IT'S BEAUTIFUL IN JUNE WHEN THE IRISES INSIDE BLOOM THOUGH...
FORGET IT, IT'S NOT JUNE NOW.

WE DIDN'T WANT TO PAY FOR THE GARDEN SO WE CONTINUED WALKING TO THE SHRINE.

THERE IS A BIG GATE AT THE SHRINE'S ENTRANCE.
THIS IS CALLED A "TORII" GATE.
IT SEPARATES OUR EARTHLY WORLD FROM THE SACRED GROUND.

YOU HAVE TO GIVE A BOW OF RESPECT TO INFORM THE GODS THAT YOU'RE GOING IN TO PRAY.
OH...
BUT MOST FOREIGNERS DON'T KNOW THIS AND JUST GO IN WITHOUT BOWING.

LET ME EXPLAIN HOW TO PURIFY YOURSELF AND PRAY AT A SHINTO SHRINE...

THE ACTUAL PRAYING IS ALSO COMPLICATED...

① THROW YOUR COINS INTO THE OFFERING BOX.
五円
5 YEN IS CALLED "GOEN" IN JAPANESE, WHICH MEANS LUCK OR FATE, SO IT IS COMMONLY USED WHEN PRAYING.

② BOW TWICE, CLAP TWICE, THEN WITH YOUR HANDS STILL TOGETHER, PRAY IN YOUR MIND.

③ AFTER PRAYING, BOW ONE MORE TIME.
OK... I THINK I'LL TEND TO MY BOY INSTEAD...

YOU CAN ALSO DO "OMIKUJI," WHICH IS TO DRAW LOTS.
IF IT'S BAD LUCK, YOU WRAP THE PAPER HERE SO THE GODS CAN HELP YOU.

THIS ONE IS CALLED "EMA," A WOODEN PLAQUE THAT YOU CAN BUY TO WRITE YOUR WISHES TO ASK THE GODS TO HELP YOU.
WHY IS EVERYTHING SO COMPLICATED HERE?

APPARENTLY MY FAMILY DIDN'T LIKE THIS PLACE THOUGH I ENJOYED IT WHEN I CAME WITH MY FRIENDS. IF YOU VISIT ON A WEEKEND YOU MIGHT SEE A TRADITIONAL JAPANESE WEDDING CEREMONY.

A VISIT TO ASAKUSA

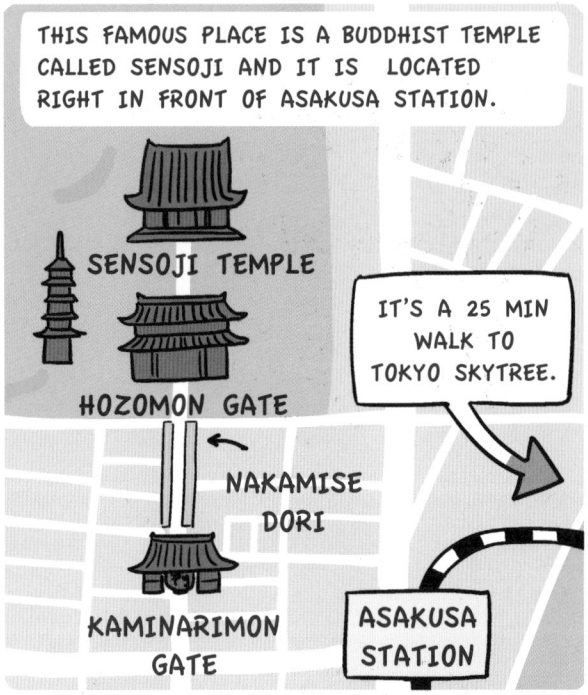

THESE GOOD LUCK CHARMS ARE SOLD AT BOTH SHRINES AND TEMPLES. BUT THEY ARE BELIEVED TO STOP WORKING AFTER A YEAR BECAUSE THEY BECOME TOO SATURATED WITH ALL THE BAD LUCK THEY'VE ABSORBED FOR YOU.

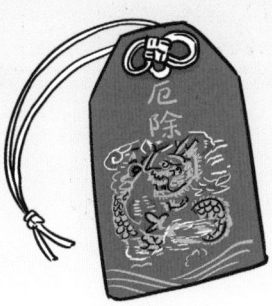

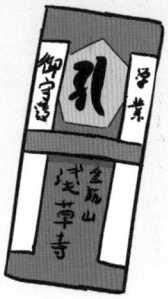

SINCE WE ARE DONE WITH THE TEMPLE, WHY DON'T WE GO TO THE VISITOR CENTER? YOU CAN CATCH A BIRD'S EYE VIEW OF THE TEMPLE TOO.
REALLY? LET'S GO!
THE ASAKUSA VISITOR CENTER LOOKS FUNKY!
THERE'S A LOT OF TOURIST INFORMATION HERE.
THERE'S INFO ABOUT YUKATA, DANCE AND EVEN A NINJA EXPERIENCE!
HERE'S THE LIFT. LET'S GO UP TO THE TOP FLOOR.
THERE'S A NICE CAFE HERE TOO.
OH! I CAN SEE THE TEMPLE DOWN THERE!
I CAN SEE TOKYO SKYTREE OVER HERE!
OK, THAT'S ENOUGH SIGHT-SEEING...
WE'RE HUNGRY...
THERE ARE 2 RESTAURANTS THAT I RECOMMEND.

"KIKKO" SERVES JAPANESE SET MEALS AND THEY PERFORM LIVE SHAMISEN MUSIC WHILE YOU EAT.

WHAT'S A SHAMISEN?
IT'S A KIND OF TRADITIONAL JAPANESE STRING INSTRUMENT.

WHAT'S THE OTHER PLACE?
THE OTHER PLACE IS CALLED ASAKUSA IMAHAN.

THEY SERVE AWESOME MOUTH-WATERING SUKIYAKI USING TOP QUALITY BEEF.

THEIR WAITRESSES ARE ALSO DRESSED IN KIMONO AND YOU CAN TAKE PHOTOS WITH THEM!

BOTH ARE A BIT PRICEY BUT THEY PROVIDE A VERY NICE TRADITIONAL JAPANESE DINING EXPERIENCE.
MY SON IS TOO YOUNG TO APPRECIATE MUSIC SO LET'S GO EAT BEEF INSTEAD.

LOOKS LIKE ASAKUSA IS A GREAT PLACE FOR FAMILIES WITH KIDS.

A KIMONO MAKEOVER IN ASAKUSA

STUDIO NANAIRO: nana-iro.tokyo/en/

AFTER CHOOSING MY OUTFIT, I WENT TO CHANGE INTO THEIR INNER GARMENTS AND WHITE ROBE.

THEY EVEN PROVIDED THE TRADITIONAL JAPANESE WHITE SOCKS CALLED "TABI" TO WEAR WITH THE KIMONO.

THEY ALSO GAVE ME A CLEAR PLASTIC TOTE BAG WITH A BOTTLE OF MINERAL WATER AND SPACE FOR MY PHONE.

HOW THOUGHTFUL!

THE DRESSING ROOM WAS VERY SPACIOUS. THE MAKEUP ARTIST AND HAIR STYLIST WORKED SIMULTANEOUSLY ON ME.

THE HAIR STYLIST PUT WARM CURLERS IN MY HAIR SO IT WOULD FIT INTO THE WIG LATER.

I LOOK LIKE A GRANNY NOW...

THE MAKEUP BECAME HEAVIER AS THICK EYEBROWS AND FAKE EYELASHES WERE ADDED.

AHAHAHA! YOUR EYEBROWS LOOK LIKE CRAYON SHIN-CHAN NOW!

THIS IS CRAYON SHIN-CHAN

...

THE UNCOMFORTABLE PART WAS PUTTING ON THE HEAVY WIG AND HAVING THE STYLIST INSERT THE ACCESSORIES INTO ANY EMPTY PLOT OF GRASSLAND SHE COULD FIND...

MY NECK BECAME REALLY TIRED...

NO PHOTOS ARE ALLOWED IN THE STUDIO EXCEPT RIGHT OUTSIDE THE SHOOTING AREA.

PUTTING ON THE KIMONO WAS LIKE WRAPPING A PRESENT WITH MANY LAYERS...

I NOW KNOW WHY JAPANESE GIRLS ARE SO SLIM...

YOU DON'T FEEL LIKE EATING ANYTHING AFTER YOUR TUMMY IS ALL WRAPPED UP!
AND IT'S HEAVY TOO!
HA HA!

FINALLY WE WENT INTO THE PHOTO-SHOOTING AREA. THE PHOTOGRAPHER AND HIS ASSISTANT WERE ALREADY THERE.
GOOD AFTERNOON!
GOOD AFTERNOON!

THE PHOTOGRAPHER WAS VERY PROFESSIONAL AND GAVE CLEAR INSTRUCTIONS.
LOOK OVER THERE AND TUCK IN YOUR CHIN, SMILE A BIT, NO TEETH.

THE PHOTOS WERE ALMOST IMMEDIATELY TRANSFERRED INTO THE LAPTOP WHERE HE CHECKED AND INSTRUCTED THE STYLIST TO ADJUST WHERE REQUIRED.
HMM.. MORE BLUSH HERE.
OK!

WE DID A TOTAL OF 5 POSES USING 4 DIFFERENT PROPS:
THE FOX MASK WAS MY FAVORITE BECAUSE IT IS CUTE AND MYSTERIOUS.

STUDIO NANAIRO: nana-iro.tokyo/en/

A STROLL AROUND UENO

THERE ARE LOTS OF THINGS TO SEE IN UENO, SO I'LL JUST INTRODUCE THE ONES THAT I THINK ARE WORTH VISITING IF YOU ONLY HAVE ONE DAY THERE:

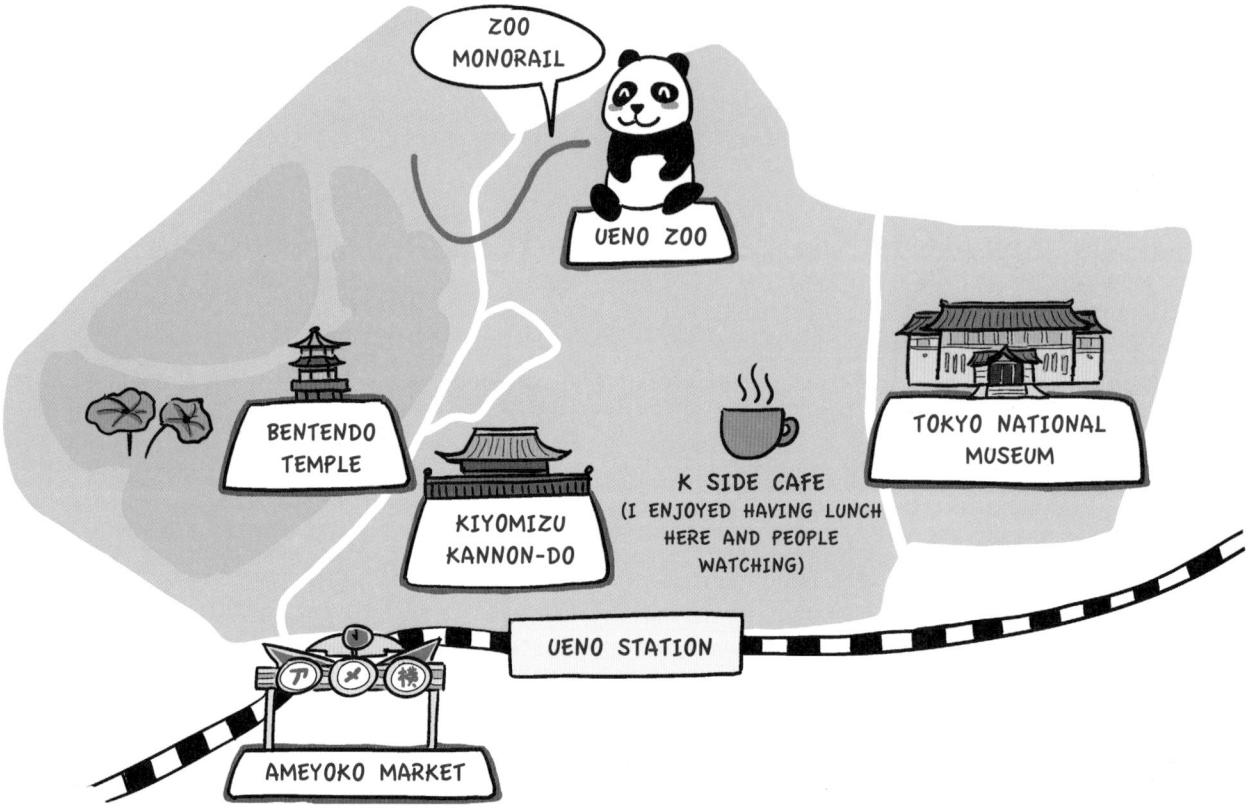

UENO ZOO IS A WORLD-CLASS ZOO AND THE OLDEST ONE IN JAPAN. IT IS SO BIG THAT YOU CAN EASILY SPEND HALF A DAY THERE.
ITS MAIN ATTRACTION IS THE CUTE PANDA!

BUT IT IS VERY BUSY WHENEVER THE PANDA IS FACING THE CROWD...

THE ZOO IS WELL-KEPT, CLEAN AND HAS CLEAR SIGNS FOR GETTING AROUND.
YOU CAN ALSO GET A ZOO PAMPHLET IN ENGLISH.

THERE'S NOT MUCH DISTANCE BETWEEN YOU AND THE ANIMALS SO YOU CAN GET A REALLY GOOD VIEW.

IN FACT, I GOT EXTREMELY CLOSE TO A SHOEBILL STORK THAT DIDN'T MOVE MUCH. EVERYONE THOUGHT I TOOK A PHOTO OF A STATUE!
I'M SO HANDSOME, RIGHT?

I WAS RUSHED FOR TIME SO I TOOK THE MONORAIL TO THE WEST SIDE OF THE ZOO.
YOU CAN WALK IF YOU WANT TO SAVE THE MONEY!

LASTLY I WANT TO MENTION THE TOKYO NATIONAL MUSEUM.
IT'S SO BIG THAT I COULD HAVE SPENT THE ENTIRE DAY THERE!

THE EXHIBITS FOCUS ON JAPANESE TRADITIONAL AND RELIGIOUS ART...
...LIKE CALLIGRAPHY AND PAINTING.

THERE ARE ALSO LOTS OF SAMURAI SUITS OF ARMOR AND SWORDS.
WOW! THE DETAILS!

AND OF COURSE, BEAUTIFUL KIMONOS.

THERE ARE 4 BUILDINGS WITH PERMANENT EXHIBITS BUT I ONLY MANAGED TO SEE THE MAIN BUILDING.
SORRY, WE ARE CLOSING SOON...
I RAN OUT OF TIME!
OH MY GOD!

I'LL SPEND MORE TIME IN UENO ON MY NEXT TRIP.

VISITING A HOT SPRING BATH IN ODAIBA

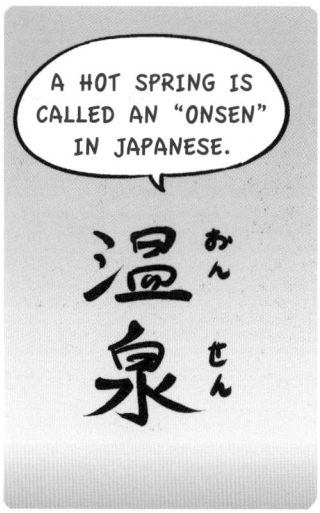

ONCE INSIDE, YOU HAVE TO TAKE OFF YOUR SHOES AND STORE THEM IN A SHOE LOCKER.

IT'S TOO SMALL FOR BOOTS THOUGH.

THEN YOU GO TO THE RECEPTION COUNTER TO REGISTER AND COLLECT ANOTHER LOCKER KEY TO STORE YOUR BAGS AND CLOTHES.

THIS LOCKER KEY IS ATTACHED TO A WRISTBAND SO YOU WEAR IT WHEREVER YOU GO. ANY PURCHASES INSIDE ARE CHARGED TO YOUR ASSIGNED LOCKER NUMBER.

SO I HAVE 2 KEYS NOW...

OEDO-ONSEN PROVIDES A YUKATA AND THERE ARE MANY COLORS TO CHOOSE FROM.

I'LL HAVE THE PINK YUKATA SIZE M WITH A PURPLE OBI PLEASE.

男性 Men

女性 Women

A YUKATA IS A CASUAL AND THINNER VERSION OF A KIMONO.

IT CONSISTS OF JUST A COTTON ROBE.

AND A CLOTH BELT CALLED AN "OBI."

ONLY WEAR YOUR UNDERWEAR UNDER IT. (YOU SHOULDN'T BE COMPLETELY NAKED OR WEARING OTHER CLOTHES...)

AFTER FINDING MY ASSIGNED LOCKER IN THE WOMAN'S CHANGING ROOM, I HAD TO CHANGE ON THE SPOT.

A BIT EMBARRASSING WITH OTHERS AROUND...

WHEN YOU PUT ON A YUKATA, YOU HAVE TO BE CAREFUL WHICH SIDE OVERLAPS.
THE LEFT SIDE SHOULD BE ON TOP.
THE OTHER WAY IS FOR DRESSING CORPSES.

AFTER PUTTING ON YOUR YUKATA, YOU CAN PROCEED TO THE MAIN HALL.
I ALWAYS CARRY A SMALL WATERPROOF BAG THAT CONTAINS MY COMB, GLASSES CASE AND PHONE. YOU CAN BUY THEM FROM DEPARTMENT STORES.

THERE ARE LOTS OF FOOD AND DRINK STALLS INSIDE THE MAIN HALL, WHERE YOU CAN MEET YOUR FRIENDS AND ENJOY FREE-FLOW WATER AND HOT TEA.
I LIKE HOW THEY DECORATED THIS PLACE TO LOOK LIKE THE OLDEN DAYS...

THERE WERE SOME TRADITIONAL JAPANESE GAMES TOO.
BUT IF YOU WANT TO PLAY THEM YOU'LL HAVE TO PAY EXTRA.

I PREFER TO SOAK IN THE HOT SPRING FIRST BEFORE EATING. YOU CAN COLLECT A SMALL AND A BIG TOWEL AT THE DRESSING ROOM FOR THE LARGE BATH.
THANK YOU!

THERE ARE LOCKERS INSIDE WHERE YOU CAN SAFELY STORE YOUR YUKATA, UNDERWEAR, AND ANY OF YOUR OTHER STUFF.
HOPE NOBODY IS LOOKING.

IF YOU FEEL SHY WALKING AROUND NAKED, YOU CAN USE THE SMALL TOWEL TO COVER UP WHEN YOU ARE GOING INTO THE MAIN BATH HALL.

THE BATH HALL IS VERY BIG WITH SEVERAL POOLS OF HOT SPRING WATER AT DIFFERENT DEPTHS AND TEMPERATURES.

BEFORE DIPPING INTO THE BATH THOUGH, YOU NEED TO WASH YOURSELF UNTIL YOU'RE CLEAN.
BODY WASH, SHAMPOO AND CONDITIONER ARE ALL PROVIDED!

IF YOU HAVE LONG HAIR, YOU NEED TO TIE IT UP AND NOT LET IT TOUCH THE WATER.

AS FOR THE SMALL TOWEL, YOU CAN PUT IT AT THE SIDE OF THE POOL OR ON YOUR HEAD BUT NEVER DIP IT IN THE WATER.
I PUT IT ON MY HEAD TO WIPE OFF THE SWEAT...

IF YOU FEEL LIKE BATHING OUTDOORS, THERE ARE POOLS AND SMALL TUBS IN THE GARDEN TOO.
THOUGH I GOT PRETTY BORED BY MYSELF...

WHEN YOU'RE DONE, YOU CAN RINSE YOURSELF IN THE SHOWER OR JUST LEAVE THE GOODNESS OF THE HOT SPRING MINERALS ON YOU.
YOUR SKIN SHOULD FEEL VERY SMOOTH.

THE DRESSING ROOM IS VERY WELL EQUIPPED WITH A BASIN IN ALMOST EVERY CUBICLE FOR WASHING YOUR FACE.

THEY HAVE ALL THE SKINCARE AND HAIRCARE PRODUCTS, RIGHT DOWN TO BLOW-DRY LOTION TO PROTECT YOUR HAIR FROM THE HAIR DRYER'S HEAT.

AFTER EATING, I WENT TO THE OPEN-AIR FOOT BATH THAT HAS A VERY LONG PEBBLED PATH FOR YOU TO WALK ON AND MASSAGE YOUR FEET.
OUCH!

I ENJOYED THIS ONSEN BUT I RECOMMEND GOING WITH FRIENDS SO YOU WON'T GET BORED AND WILL STAY LONGER.
ZZZ...

GARDENS AND NATURE WALKS

THERE ARE MANY LARGE AND SMALL PARKS IN TOKYO, MOST OF WHICH ARE FREE BUT THERE ARE A FEW THAT CHARGE AN ENTRANCE FEE, SUCH AS SHINJUKU GYOEN AND RIKUGIEN.

IF YOU LIKE TO HIKE, YOU CAN TAKE THE CHUO LINE TRAIN FOR A DAY TRIP TO EITHER MT. TAKAO OR OKUTAMA.
THEY ARE LOCATED SLIGHTLY OUTSIDE OF TOKYO.

MT. TAKAO, OR TAKAOSAN, IS FAMOUS FOR ITS AUTUMN LEAVES AND EASY HIKING TRAIL.
YOU CAN ALSO TAKE THE CABLE CAR IF YOU DON'T WANT TO WALK.

OKUTAMA IS FAMOUS FOR ITS BEAUTIFUL RIVER LANDSCAPE BUT IT IS FURTHER AWAY FROM THE CITY THAN TAKAOSAN.

IF YOU LIKE TO SEE TEMPLES AND THE SEA, YOU CAN VISIT KAMAKURA, FAMOUS FOR ITS GIANT BUDDHA STATUE.
IT CAN BE A DAY TRIP TOO. BUT A BIT RUSHED.

ALTHOUGH MT. FUJI. ISN'T IN TOKYO, IT'S JUST A FEW HOURS DRIVE AWAY.
IT'S ALSO A UNESCO WORLD HERITAGE SITE.

...AND BECAUSE MT. FUJI IS SO FAMOUS AND HIGHLY ACCESSIBLE FROM TOKYO, I'M GOING TO COVER THE GORGEOUS MOUNTAIN IN DETAIL.

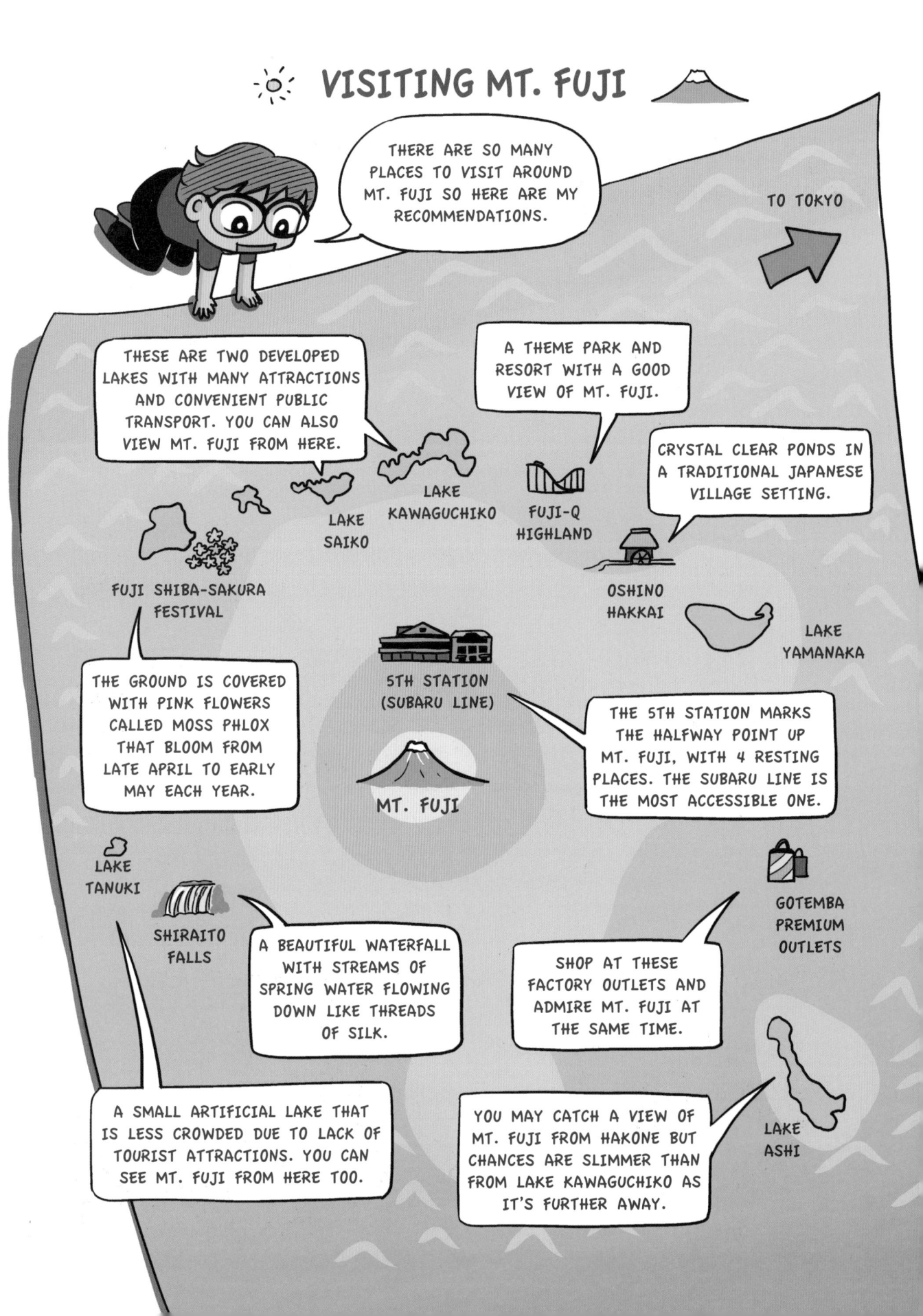
VISITING MT. FUJI
THERE ARE SO MANY PLACES TO VISIT AROUND MT. FUJI SO HERE ARE MY RECOMMENDATIONS.
TO TOKYO
THESE ARE TWO DEVELOPED LAKES WITH MANY ATTRACTIONS AND CONVENIENT PUBLIC TRANSPORT. YOU CAN ALSO VIEW MT. FUJI FROM HERE.
A THEME PARK AND RESORT WITH A GOOD VIEW OF MT. FUJI.
CRYSTAL CLEAR PONDS IN A TRADITIONAL JAPANESE VILLAGE SETTING.
LAKE SAIKO
LAKE KAWAGUCHIKO
FUJI-Q HIGHLAND
FUJI SHIBA-SAKURA FESTIVAL
OSHINO HAKKAI
LAKE YAMANAKA
THE GROUND IS COVERED WITH PINK FLOWERS CALLED MOSS PHLOX THAT BLOOM FROM LATE APRIL TO EARLY MAY EACH YEAR.
5TH STATION (SUBARU LINE)
THE 5TH STATION MARKS THE HALFWAY POINT UP MT. FUJI, WITH 4 RESTING PLACES. THE SUBARU LINE IS THE MOST ACCESSIBLE ONE.
MT. FUJI
LAKE TANUKI
SHIRAITO FALLS
A BEAUTIFUL WATERFALL WITH STREAMS OF SPRING WATER FLOWING DOWN LIKE THREADS OF SILK.
GOTEMBA PREMIUM OUTLETS
SHOP AT THESE FACTORY OUTLETS AND ADMIRE MT. FUJI AT THE SAME TIME.
A SMALL ARTIFICIAL LAKE THAT IS LESS CROWDED DUE TO LACK OF TOURIST ATTRACTIONS. YOU CAN SEE MT. FUJI FROM HERE TOO.
YOU MAY CATCH A VIEW OF MT. FUJI FROM HAKONE BUT CHANCES ARE SLIMMER THAN FROM LAKE KAWAGUCHIKO AS IT'S FURTHER AWAY.
LAKE ASHI

GETTING TO THE MT. FUJI AREA FROM TOKYO

BY TRAIN
2-3 HOURS

YOU CAN BUY SINGLE TRIP TICKETS OR A 2-3 DAY PASS FROM EITHER JR OR ODAKYU TRAIN LINES. BOTH OF THEM HAVE SALES OFFICES AT SHINJUKU STATION. THE JOURNEY TAKES 3 HOURS BY JR LOCAL TRAIN WHICH IS SLIGHTLY CHEAPER, BUT ONLY 2 HOURS BY THE JR KAIJI LIMITED EXPRESS SERVICE OR ODAKYU'S ROMANCECAR.

BY HIGHWAY BUS
2 HOURS

HIGHWAY BUSES ARE ECONOMICAL FOR A 1-2 DAY TRIP TO A SINGLE LOCATION. THERE ARE FREQUENT DEPARTURES FROM SHINJUKU HIGHWAY BUS TERMINAL. BUT IF YOU TRAVEL DURING PEAK PERIODS THERE MAY BE JAMS AND IT CAN TAKE MORE THAN 3 HOURS.

THE FOUR SEASONS OF MT. FUJI

SPRING
MAR-MAY

THE FUJI SHIBA-SAKURA FESTIVAL IS IN LATE APRIL/ EARLY MAY, WHEN PINK MOSS PHLOX CARPETS THE LANDSCAPE. TAKE THE BUS FROM KAWAGUCHIKO STATION.

SUMMER
JUN-SEP

THE OFFICIAL CLIMBING SEASON IS FROM EARLY JULY TO MID-SEPTEMBER. THERE ARE PLENTY OF THINGS TO DO AND SEE EVEN IF YOU ARE NOT CLIMBING MT. FUJI.

FALL
OCT-NOV

CATCH RED MAPLE LEAVES AND MT. FUJI FROM THE MAPLE CORRIDOR OR MT. KOYODAI. BOTH ARE NEAR LAKE KAWAGUCHIKO. THE BEST TIME IS IN THE MORNING BEFORE CLOUDS COVER THE MOUNTAIN.

WINTER
DEC-FEB

PICTURESQUE MT. FUJI AND THE NEARBY JAPAN ALPS ARE SNOW-CAPPED AGAINST THE CLEAR BLUE SKY.

ALTHOUGH YOU CAN MAKE A DAY TRIP TO EITHER LAKE KAWAGUCHIKO OR HAKONE, I WOULD RECOMMEND STAYING AT LEAST ONE NIGHT TO ENJOY THE LOCAL HOT SPRINGS AND FOOD.

"HOUTOU" IS A LOCAL DISH FOUND AROUND LAKE KAWAGUCHIKO, MADE OF FLAT UDON NOODLES STEWED WITH VEGETABLES IN MISO SOUP. I PERSONALLY DON'T LIKE IT BUT MAYBE YOU WILL.

LAKE KAWAGUCHIKO AREA

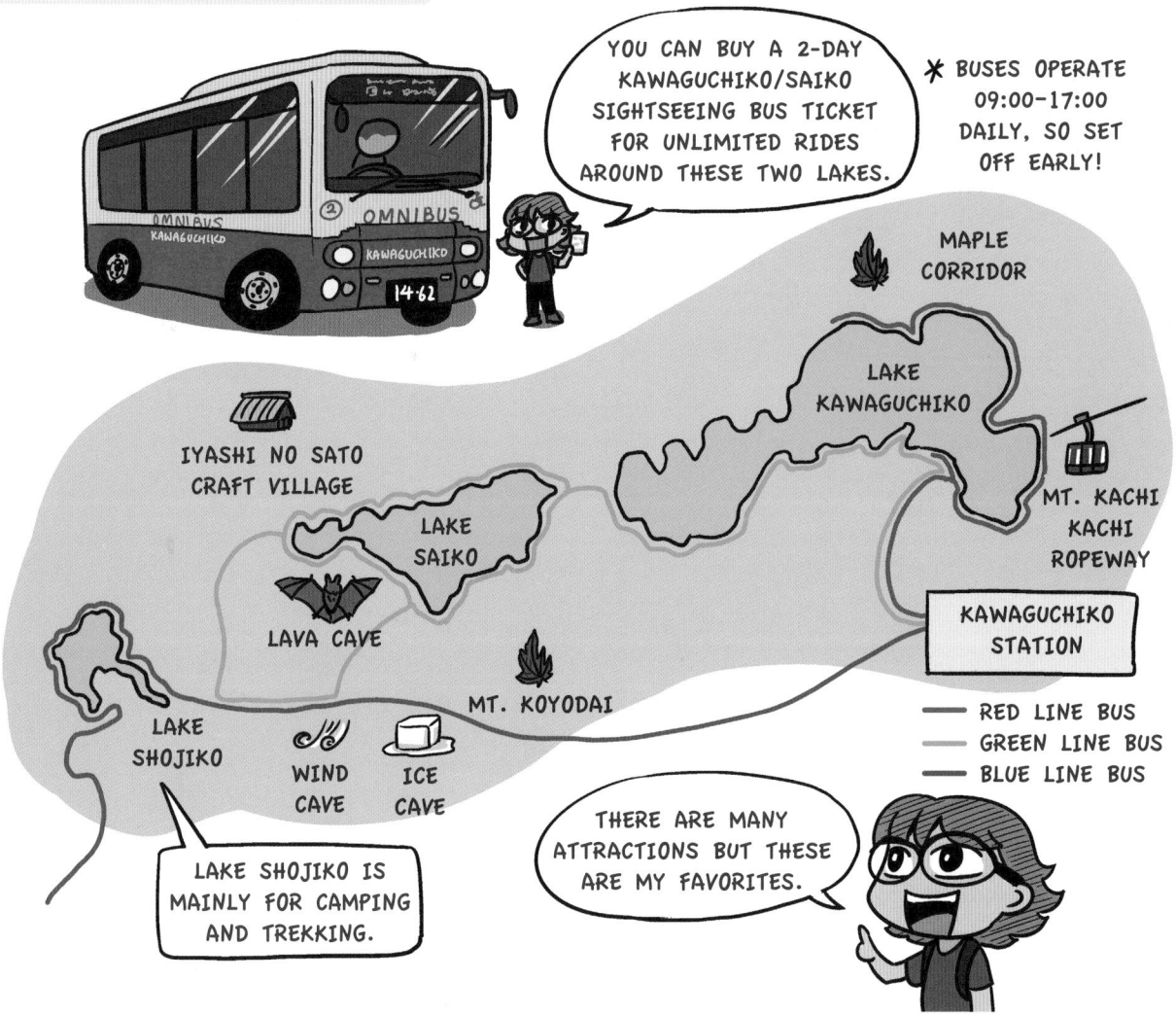

FROM HERE, YOU CAN ALSO WALK FOR A FURTHER 15 MINUTES TO THE ACTUAL PEAK OF MT. TENJO.
THERE'S ALSO A PATH TO MT. MITSUTOGE.

THERE IS A SIGN THAT SAYS IT TAKES 6 HOURS FOR A ROUND TRIP TO MT. MITSUTOGE.
BUT I THINK IT WOULD TAKE ME LONGER!

THE TRAIL ALSO GETS UNEVEN AND SLIPPERY AT THE TOP SO I SUGGEST WEARING A GOOD PAIR OF HIKING SHOES.

THERE'S A SHRINE UP HERE WITH A REALLY GREAT VIEW OF MT. FUJI BUT I WAS IN A RUSH THE DAY I DID THE TRIP SO UNFORTUNATELY I HAD TO SKIP IT.

YOU CAN EITHER COME BACK DOWN BY ROPEWAY OR HIKE DOWN IN 30 MIN.
I TOOK THE ROPEWAY TO SAVE TIME!

THE NEXT ATTRACTION I RECOMMEND IS IYASHI NO SATO CRAFT VILLAGE, LOCATED AT LAKE SAIKO.
IT'S A SMALL RECONSTRUCTION OF A TRADITIONAL JAPANESE VILLAGE.
IT'S SIMILAR TO THE NEARBY VILLAGE OF OSHINO HAKKAI, ANOTHER MT. FUJI TOURIST SPOT, BUT IT'S MUCH LESS CROWDED.

YOU CAN CATCH A GLIMPSE OF MT. FUJI FROM HERE TOO!
HERE

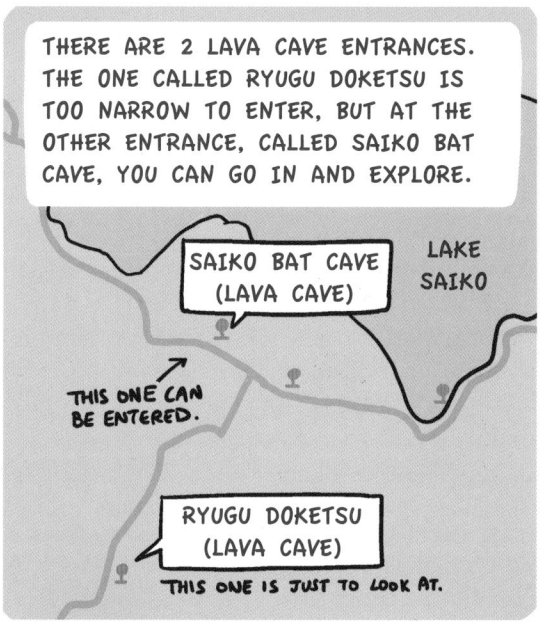

A "POWER SPOT" FOR THE JAPANESE IS A SPIRITUAL PLACE WHERE YOU CAN RECEIVE SPECIAL ENERGY TO FEEL GOOD.

BUT IF YOU'RE RUSHING, I RECOMMEND SKIPPING THIS ENTRANCE AND GOING TO THE OTHER ONE, WHICH YOU PAY A FEE TO ENTER.
YOU'LL NEED TO WALK A BIT TO THE ACTUAL CAVE ENTRANCE THOUGH.

HELMETS ARE PROVIDED BECAUSE CERTAIN SECTIONS HAVE A VERY LOW CEILING WITH WATER CONSTANTLY DRIPPING DOWN EVEN THOUGH IT WASN'T RAINING OUTSIDE.
YOU HAVE TO CRAWL THROUGH SOME PARTS TOO!

THE LAVA CAVE IS ALSO CALLED THE BAT CAVE. SOME SECTIONS ARE CLOSED OFF TO PROTECT THE BATS THAT LIVE THERE.

AFTER YOU'VE SEEN THE CAVE, YOU CAN VISIT THE MINI AQUARIUM BACK AT THE TICKET OFFICE.

IT HOUSES A NEARLY EXTINCT LOCAL BLACK SALMON CALLED KUNIMASU.
BUT LOCALS SAY THIS SALMON DOESN'T TASTE GOOD...

THE NEXT PLACE YOU CAN VISIT IS THE WIND CAVE (SEE MAP ON PAGE 40).
TAKE THE GREEN LINE BUS FROM THE LAVA CAVE THEN WALK TO THE CAVE ENTRANCE.

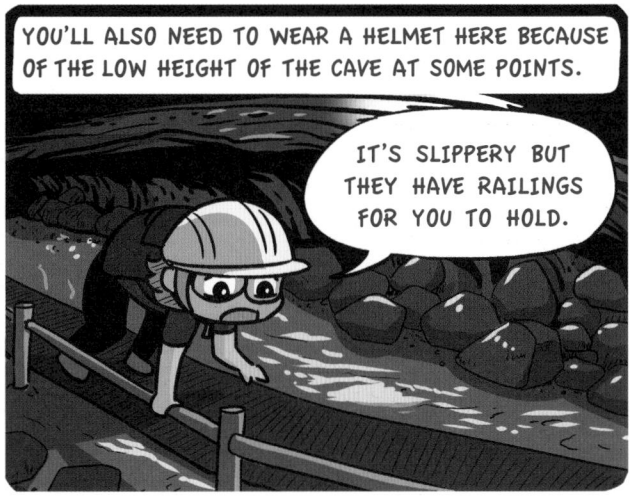
YOU'LL ALSO NEED TO WEAR A HELMET HERE BECAUSE OF THE LOW HEIGHT OF THE CAVE AT SOME POINTS.
IT'S SLIPPERY BUT THEY HAVE RAILINGS FOR YOU TO HOLD.

WIND CAVE AND ICE CAVE: mtfuji-cave.com

THE SUN AND MOON CLUB RESORT, LAKE TANUKI

THE SUN AND MOON CLUB RESORT: hitsuki-club.com

CHAPTER 2
ANIMANGA* TOKYO
* = ANIME + MANGA
MANY OF US GO TO JAPAN BECAUSE OF OUR LOVE OF ANIME AND MANGA.
IN CASE YOU DON'T KNOW, ANIME MEANS ANIMATION...
AND MANGA MEANS COMICS.
I ENJOY READING MANGA BECAUSE THEY USE PICTURE PANELS RATHER THAN WORDS TO CONVEY ACTION AND THE PASSING OF TIME. THIS MAKES THE STORY MORE DRAMATIC, ALMOST AS IF YOU'RE WATCHING A MOVIE.
ANIMANGA ALSO COVERS A BROAD RANGE OF THEMES...
FROM MAKING SUSHI...
TO SUPER ROBOT BATTLES...
TO COLLECTING MONSTERS...

UNLIKE THE WEST, WHERE COMICS EXIST MAINLY AS BOOKS, THE JAPANESE ARE ABLE TO EXTEND THESE FICTITIOUS WORLDS TO THEIR REAL LIVES.

THEY PRODUCE GOODS SUCH AS TOYS, SHIRTS, SNACKS, AND THEY EVEN PRINT SEXY ANIME GIRLS ONTO GIANT PILLOWS CALLED DAKIMAKURA.

OH, THIS IS MY OTAKU FRIEND.

"OTAKU" IS THE JAPANESE WORD FOR GEEK—SOMEONE OBSESSED WITH A HOBBY, USUALLY ANIMANGA-RELATED TO THE POINT OF SELDOM LEAVING HOME.

UMM... ACTUALLY I STILL GO TO WORK AND SOMETIMES I EVEN GO TO THE GYM...

THE JAPANESE ALSO HOLD EXHIBITIONS OR EVEN BUILD A WHOLE MUSEUM JUST TO SHOWCASE A SINGLE ANIMANGA TITLE OR PRODUCTION COMPANY.

EVEN IF YOU'RE NOT A FAN, YOU'LL STILL BE AMAZED AT HOW SKILLFULLY THE JAPANESE USE STORYTELLING AND DESIGN TO CREATE A UNIQUE EXPERIENCE (MAINLY TO ENTICE YOU TO SPEND $$$).

LET'S HOPE I DON'T BLOW ALL MY BUDGET IN ONE GO...

NOW WHO'S THE OTAKU?

OTAKU PARADISE AKIHABARA

THERE IS SOMETHING FOR EVERY ANIME AND MANGA LOVER HERE:

DOLLS AND THEIR ACCESSORIES

UFO DOLL CATCHERS
UFO CATCHER

GASHAPON CAPSULE TOYS
YOU INSERT COINS TO GET RANDOM TOYS CONTAINED IN CAPSULES.

ONE OF MY FRIENDS FROM MY HOME COUNTRY WANTED ME TO BRING HIM TO AKIBA BECAUSE I COULD SPEAK JAPANESE.
I JUST WANT TO TAKE A LOOK AND I WON'T BE BUYING ANYTHING.
REALLY? OK.

IT WAS A BIG MISTAKE. EVERY SHOP WE WENT IN, HE WAS LIKE A DOG RUNNING LOOSE...
WOW! I PLAYED THIS WHEN I WAS A KID!

MOST SHOPS DON'T ALLOW PHOTOGRAPHY SO WE WERE TOLD OFF SEVERAL TIMES...
NO PHOTO!
SORRY.

EVENTUALLY WE SPENT 5 HOURS IN AKIBA. HE DIDN'T BUY ANYTHING BUT HE TOOK PHOTOS OF ALMOST EVERYTHING HE SAW...
I STOOD FOR SO LONG MY LEGS HURT...

SO HERE ARE SOME OF THE SHOPS WE POPPED INTO OR I RECOMMEND.

① KOTOBUKIYA

KOTOBUKIYA IS FAMOUS FOR THEIR ACTION FIGURES AND PLASTIC MODELS. THEIR PRODUCTS ARE REALLY GOOD QUALITY.

② AKIBA CULTURES ZONE

A LARGE COLLECTION OF BOTH NEW AND PRE-OWNED COSPLAY COSTUMES, WIGS AND ACCESSORIES INCLUDING CAT PAWS! THERE ARE RENTAL SHOWCASES TOO.

③ AKIHABARA GAMERS

THEY SELL COMICS, MAGAZINES, CDS, DVDS, PC GAMES AND VOICE-ACTOR GOODS.

GRAB AN ENGLISH MAP AT THE AKIHABARA ELECTRIC TOWN EXIT OF THE STATION.

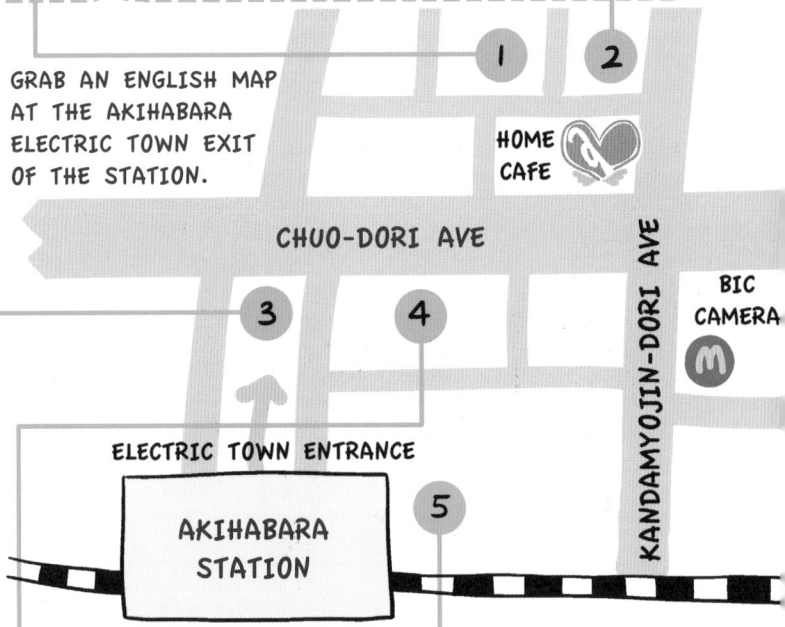

④ ANIME PLAZA

THERE IS A LARGE RENTAL SHOWCASE ON SECOND FLOOR THAT SELLS MANY PRE-OWNED TOYS AND FIGURINES.

⑤ GUNDAM CAFE

A MUST-VISIT FOR ALL GUNDAM FANS BECAUSE OF THE WAY THEY DECORATE THE FOOD AND THE LATTES. IT IS LOCATED RIGHT NEXT TO AKIHABARA STATION.

⑥ MANDARAKE

WELL-KNOWN FOR SELLING PRE-OWNED ANIME GOODS, MANGA AND ART BOOKS. A MUST-VISIT IF YOU ARE LOOKING FOR OLD TREASURES!

⑦ RETRO GAME CAMP

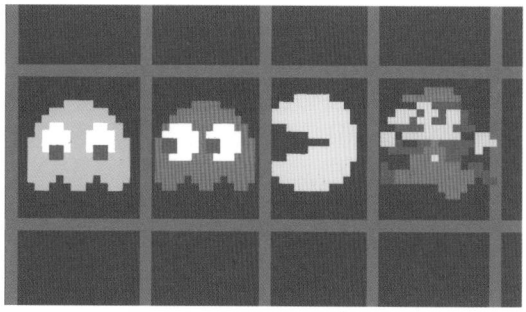

THEY SELL LOTS OF OLDER PRE-OWNED GAMES AND GAME CONSOLES.

6

7

8

9

10

HOME CAFE

AKIBA-TASHIRO LANE

AKIHABARA UDX

(AKIHABARA URBAN DEVELOPMENT X)

⑧ GACHAPON KAIKAN

IF YOU LIKE GASHAPON CAPSULE TOYS, YOU WILL LOVE THIS PLACE!

⑨ ANIMATE

animate

ANIMATE SELLS A WIDE VARIETY OF ANIME GOODS SUCH AS COMICS, NOVELS, ANIME MAGAZINES AND ACTION FIGURES AS WELL AS AUDIO AND VISUAL GOODS. THEIR BRANCH IN AKIHABARA TARGETS MALE FANS WHILE THE ONE AT IKEBUKURO IS MORE FOR GIRL FANS (AKA OTOME).

⑩ DON QUIJOTE

ALSO COMMONLY KNOWN AS "DONKI" FOR SHORT. THERE ARE MANY OUTLETS ALL OVER JAPAN BUT THE ONE IN AKIHABARA SELLS MORE COSTUMES AND ALSO HAS A GAMING ARCADE AND A MAID CAFE.

VISITING AN AKIBA MAID CAFE

OH YES, PLEASE NOTE THAT THERE IS A TIME LIMIT OF ONE HOUR ONLY...
...AND YOU CAN ONLY TAKE PHOTOS OF YOUR OWN FOOD OR DRINK, NOT OF THE CAFE OR MAIDS.
DARN...

INSIDE WAS PRETTY COZY AND WE CHOSE TO SIT AT ONE OF THE TABLES.
THIS WAY PLEASE.

ALL THE MAIDS WERE WEARING UNIFORMS AND HAD SIMILAR BANGS, MAYBE TO LOOK CUTER AND YOUNGER?

LET'S ORDER THE COMBO SO WE CAN GET OUR PHOTO TAKEN WITH THE MAIDS.
OK, BUT YOU CAN HAVE MY PHOTO BECAUSE I DON'T WANT MY GIRLFRIEND TO BE JEALOUS.

HI, CAN I HAVE YOUR NAMES PLEASE?
I'M WAHYU.
I'M EVA.

THANK YOU. HERE ARE YOUR LICENSE CARDS.
LICENSE CARDS?

WOW! THEY WROTE OUR NAMES ON THESE PLASTIC CARDS!
HA HA! YOUR TITLE IS "MY PRINCESS" AND MINE IS "MY MASTER."

*An omelette stuffed with rice and topped with ketchup.

SHE WAS REALLY GOOD AT DRAWING CATS.
WOW!

NOW WE WILL PREPARE THE STRAWBERRY MILKSHAKE!
AND TO MAKE THE DRINKS MORE DELICIOUS, WE'LL CAST A SPELL!

AT THE END OF THE SPELL, WE NEED TO MAKE A HEART SHAPE WITH OUR HANDS AND CHANT "OISHIKU NARE!"
...
OISHIKU NARE MEANS "BECOME DELICIOUS!"

OUR MAID DID A FULL DEMONSTRATION BEFORE WE OFFICIALLY STARTED THE WEIRD SPELL.
HURI HURI SHAKA SHAKA MOE MOE...
NYAN NYAN WAN WAN MOE MOE...

OISHIKU NARE!

PLEASE ENJOY YOUR DRINKS!
THANK YOU!

SO DID YOUR MILKSHAKE BECOME DELICIOUS?
NOT REALLY, IT'S A BIT TOO SWEET...
MY LATTE TOO!

THEN MY OMU RICE CAME.
WHAT WOULD YOU LIKE ME TO DRAW?
HOW ABOUT A DOG?

BUT IT TURNED OUT LOOKING MORE LIKE A KOALA BEAR...
@home cafe
BUT AT LEAST IT'S VERY CUTE!

MY FRIEND'S CURRY CAME TOO.
NOW WE HAVE TO DO A LEVEL 2 SPELL TO MAKE THE FOOD MORE DELICIOUS.
LEVEL 2?

LEVEL 2 INVOLVES SIGNIFICANTLY MORE HAND GESTURES...
KYUN KYUN, MOE MOE, BLABLABLA... (CAN'T REMEMBER)
OISHIKU NARE!

I KNOW THE SPELLS DIDN'T WORK BECAUSE THERE'S TOO MUCH KETCHUP ON MY RICE FROM THAT DRAWING SHE DID...
EVERYTHING IS TOO SWEET!

THEN SUDDENLY, MY NAME WAS CALLED.
EVA-SAMA, PLEASE COME TO THE STAGE NOW FOR YOUR PHOTO SHOOT.
OH, IT'S MY TURN!

@HOME CAFE: cafe-athome.com/en/

AN IKEBUKURO BUTLER CAFE

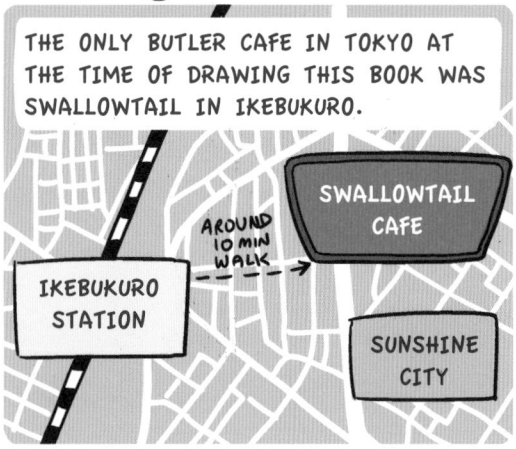

INSIDE THERE WAS ANOTHER ROUND OF GREETINGS.
WELCOME HOME OJOUSAMA!
SO MANY GUYS!

WOULD YOU LIKE US TO KEEP YOUR BAGS AND REMOVE YOUR COATS?
YES.

NOT A HANDSOME BUTLER BUT VERY GENTLEMANLY.

CAN I HOLD ON TO MY BAG?
OF COURSE YOU CAN, PLEASE KEEP YOUR VALUABLE ITEMS WITH YOU.

PLEASE LET ME ACCOMPANY YOU TO YOUR SEATS.
WOW!

HERE ARE YOUR SEATS.

I WILL PUT THE LOCKER KEYS HERE. PLEASE LET ME PUT ON NAPKINS FOR BOTH OF YOU.

IS AN ENGLISH MENU ALRIGHT?
YES, THAT WILL BE GREAT.
HE EVEN PUT A NAPKIN OVER MY BAG TO KEEP IT CLEAN.
PLEASE RING THIS BELL IF YOU NEED ANYTHING.
OK!
I THINK I'LL HAVE THE HIGH TEA SET.
I THINK I'LL HAVE THE SEAFOOD PASTA AND SALAD...
BY THE WAY, ALL THE BUTLERS HERE ARE SO SLIM!
WELL, NOT JUST ANY GUY CAN BECOME A BUTLER HERE YOU KNOW...
WE RANG THE BELL FOR OUR BUTLER TO COME AND TAKE OUR ORDER.
OUR TEA CAME PRETTY FAST.
THIS TEA CUP IS CALLED PEONY AND THIS ONE IS CALLED RED QUEEN.
WOW! DID THEY MATCH THE TEA SETS ACCORDING TO WHAT WE ARE WEARING?
YUP!

OUR BUTLER COULD SPEAK A LITTLE BIT OF ENGLISH SO HE TRIED HIS BEST TO EXPLAIN THE BUTLER CAFE CONCEPT TO US.
OJOUSAMA ARE VERY BUSY ATTENDING PARTIES EVERYDAY...
SO YOU CAN ONLY BE HERE FOR 80 MIN BEFORE RUSHING OFF TO THE NEXT PARTY.

BECAUSE YOU ARE ALWAYS PARTYING, YOU DO NOT KNOW HOW TO PAY BILLS YOURSELF...
...SO YOU MUST TAKE A TEST TO PAY YOUR OWN BILL BEFORE YOU LEAVE.

WE WILL ASK YOU TO TAKE THE TEST 20 MIN BEFORE YOU RUSH OFF TO THE NEXT PARTY.
...
UH... OK.

WOW, THEY ACTUALLY COOKED UP THIS ELABORATE STORY ABOUT THE TIME LIMIT AND PAYMENT...
VERY CREATIVE ISN'T IT?

SOON, OUR FOOD CAME.
LOOKS DELICIOUS!

OUR BUTLER TOOK DOWN A PLATE FROM MY HIGH TEA TRAY FOR ME.
PLEASE RING THE BELL IF YOU NEED ANY HELP.
OK.

BUT I ATE PRETTY FAST AND DIDN'T WANT TO WAIT FOR OUR BUTLER TO COME.
LET ME SWAP MY OWN PLATES.
I DON'T THINK HE'LL BE HAPPY...

SURE ENOUGH, OUR BUTLER SAW WHAT HAPPENED AND IMMEDIATELY DASHED OVER...
OJOUSAMA! PLEASE DON'T DO THAT YOURSELF! IT IS OUR JOB TO SERVE YOU!
WOULD YOU LIKE ME TO REFILL YOUR CUP NOW?
UH...YES PLEASE.
THEY DON'T LIKE IT IF YOU REFILL YOUR OWN CUP...
FELT SCOLDED...
AH...
WE FINISHED OUR FOOD BEFORE THE TIME WAS UP.
HEY, I WANT TO GO TO THE LADIES' ROOM.
ME TOO. LET'S RING THE BELL.
HOW MAY I HELP YOU?
WE WOULD LIKE TO GO TO THE LADIES' ROOM.
I SEE, THIS WAY PLEASE.
SEEMS HAPPY

SO THAT WAS THE END OF MY FIRST AND LAST VISIT TO A BUTLER CAFE.

AT A COSPLAY STUDIO

I ALREADY HAD A BAD FEELING WHEN I CHECKED IN ON THAT DAY...
PLEASE KINDLY MAKE PAYMENT FOR THE PACKAGE FIRST.
BUT I ALREADY PAID WHEN I BOOKED ONLINE!
OOPS, I'M SORRY! PLEASE LET ME CHECK AGAIN.

WHEN WE'D CLEARED UP THE PAYMENT PROBLEM, SHE HANDED ME A FOLDER SO I COULD SELECT MY COSTUME.
I WANT THIS MIKO (PRIESTESS) COSTUME AND WIG SO I LOOK LIKE KIKYO FROM THE INUYASHA ANIME.
LIKE THIS

I'M SORRY, BUT WE DON'T HAVE A BOW AND ARROW...
IT'S OK, I CAN USE A SWORD OR A FAN INSTEAD.

THEN SHE SHOWED ME INTO A DRESSING ROOM AND TOLD ME TO PUT ON THE COSTUME FIRST BEFORE DOING THE MAKEUP.
OK!
PLEASE LET ME KNOW WHEN YOU'RE READY.
BTW YOU CAN BUY THE SAME COSTUME FROM SHOPS FOR ONLY 3,000 YEN...

AFTER I GOT CHANGED, SHE BEGAN TO PUT ON MY MAKEUP...
OH, SO SHE'S THE RECEPTIONIST, MAKEUP ARTIST AND HAIR STYLIST!

BUT FOR SOME ODD REASON SHE MADE ME LOOK PALE AND OLD...
IS SHE TRYING TO MAKE ME INTO AN OLD MIKO?!
EYE BAGS BECAME OBVIOUS
PALE LIPS
PALE BLUSH

THEN SHE JUST LEFT THE WIG ON MY HEAD, UNCOMBED!
OMG!
I LOOK LIKE A FREAKIN' DEAD MIKO PRIESTESS!!!

WAS IT BECAUSE IT WAS NEARLY HALLOWEEN THAT SHE MADE ME LOOK LIKE A GHOST?

PLEASE LET ME KNOW WHEN WE CAN START TAKING PHOTOS, MY CAMERA IS READY.
WAIT, WHAT? SHE'S ALSO THE PHOTOGRAPHER!?

THERE WERE SOME SETUPS FOR BACKDROPS AT THE STUDIO. THERE WAS THIS SPACE THEME...

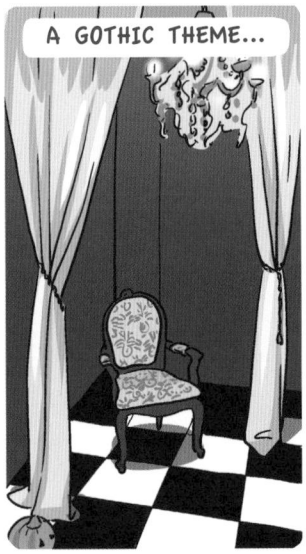
A GOTHIC THEME...

AND A TRADITIONAL JAPANESE THEME...
I'LL HAVE THIS ONE.
OK.

HOWEVER, SHORTLY AFTER WE STARTED SHOOTING, SHE NOTICED SOMETHING WRONG...
HMM... WHY DOES IT LOOK SO WEIRD...
HMM?

OH MY GOSH! YOUR FAKE EYELASH FELL OFF!!!
WHAT?

I'M SO SORRY! PLEASE LET ME GET THE GLUE TO STICK IT BACK ON.
...

AH! THIS NEW GLUE IS MUCH BETTER!
WAIT, YOU MEAN YOU TRIED TO SQUEEZE FROM AN OLD TUBE?

PLEASE DO IT NOW!
SHOULD I RE-GLUE THE OTHER EYELASH TOO OR SHOULD WE WAIT FOR IT TO DROP OFF THEN GLUE IT BACK?

AS IT WAS NEARLY HALLOWEEN, THEY HAD PUMPKINS AND SKELETONS LYING AROUND.
LET'S SHOOT WITH THESE SINCE IT'S GOING TO BE HALLOWEEN.
EH? OK...

ANOTHER REASON WAS I LOOKED DEAD ANYWAY.

NEXT TIME I'LL TRY A PLACE WITH DECORATED BACKDROPS WHERE YOU DO YOUR OWN MAKEUP, COSTUME AND PHOTOS, LIKE COSPLAY STUDIO BOOTY NEAR OJIMA STATION (TOEI SHINJUKU LINE), OR HACOSTADIUM NEAR FUNABASHI-KEIBAJO STATION (KEISEI LINE).
A JAPANESE FRIEND CAN HELP YOU READ THE WEBSITES.

TOKYO ONE PIECE TOWER

THE MANGA AND ANIME WAS SUCH A HIT IN JAPAN THAT THE INDOOR AMUSEMENT PARK "TOKYO ONE PIECE TOWER" WAS SET UP AT THE ICONIC TOKYO TOWER. YOU CAN BUY TICKETS ON THE SPOT OR IN ADVANCE ON THE WEBSITE: onepiecetower.tokyo/?lang=en.

TOKYO ONE PIECE TOWER

THE ENTRANCE TO THE PARK IS ON THE 3RD FLOOR OF TOKYO TOWER. I WENT THERE WITH WAHYU, MY OTAKU FRIEND.

THE DISTRICT OF ROPPONGI IS NEARBY (WELL-KNOWN FOR CLUBBING)

IT'S NOT FAR TO ZOZOJI, A FAMOUS AND BEAUTIFUL BUDDHIST TEMPLE IN A SMALL PARK.

THE JOURNEY BEGINS IN A GALLERY OF LCD SCREENS SHOWING IMPORTANT MOMENTS FROM THE MANGA.
THE SCREENS ARE INTERACTIVE, WITH SPECIAL EFFECTS.
オオオオ
オオオ!!!

AFTER THAT, YOU ARE IMMERSED IN THE WORLD OF "ONE PIECE" WHERE LIFE-SIZE CHARACTER FIGURINES WELCOME YOU WITH A BANQUET.
FAKE FOOD OF COURSE.

THE QUALITY OF THE MODELS WAS VERY HIGH AND NOT AT ALL SHODDY.
HEY, FAKE BEER!

TOO BAD I WAS WEARING DARK GREY AND BLENDED IN WITH THE BACKGROUND.
UM... I CAN'T SEE YOU...

WAHYU AND I HAD FUN POSING AND TAKING PHOTOS IN THAT BANQUET BALLROOM.
TOUCH HER, AND I'LL TAKE A PHOTO TO POST ONLINE!

THE 4TH FLOOR WAS MOSTLY GAME STALLS LIKE THESE:

THE BEST ATTRACTIONS WERE ON THE 5TH FLOOR:

THE EXIT WAS FILLED WITH HANDSOME GUYS WAITING FOR ME.
PLASTIC FIGURES OF COURSE.
THE HIGHLIGHT OF THE PARK WAS A LIVE SHOW CALLED "WELCOME TO TONGARI MYSTERY LOVE."
WOW IT'S LIVE ACTION!
THE ACTING IS GREAT!
WE WERE GIVEN TORCHES DESIGNED TO LOOK LIKE MAGICAL STONES SO WE COULD PASS OUR POWERS TO THE CHARACTERS ON STAGE TO FIGHT OFF EVIL.
THIS FEELS LIKE DISNEY CHANNEL...
THE LIVE SHOWS ARE UPDATED FROM TIME TO TIME.
THE COSTUMES, ACTING, STAGE AND LIGHTING EFFECTS WERE ALL AWESOME!
WE SPENT A GOOD 3 HOURS THERE AND TOOK LOTS OF MEMORABLE SHOTS.
I WISH I'D WORN SOMETHING BRIGHTER!!!
HA HA!

THE GUNDAM STATUE IN ODAIBA

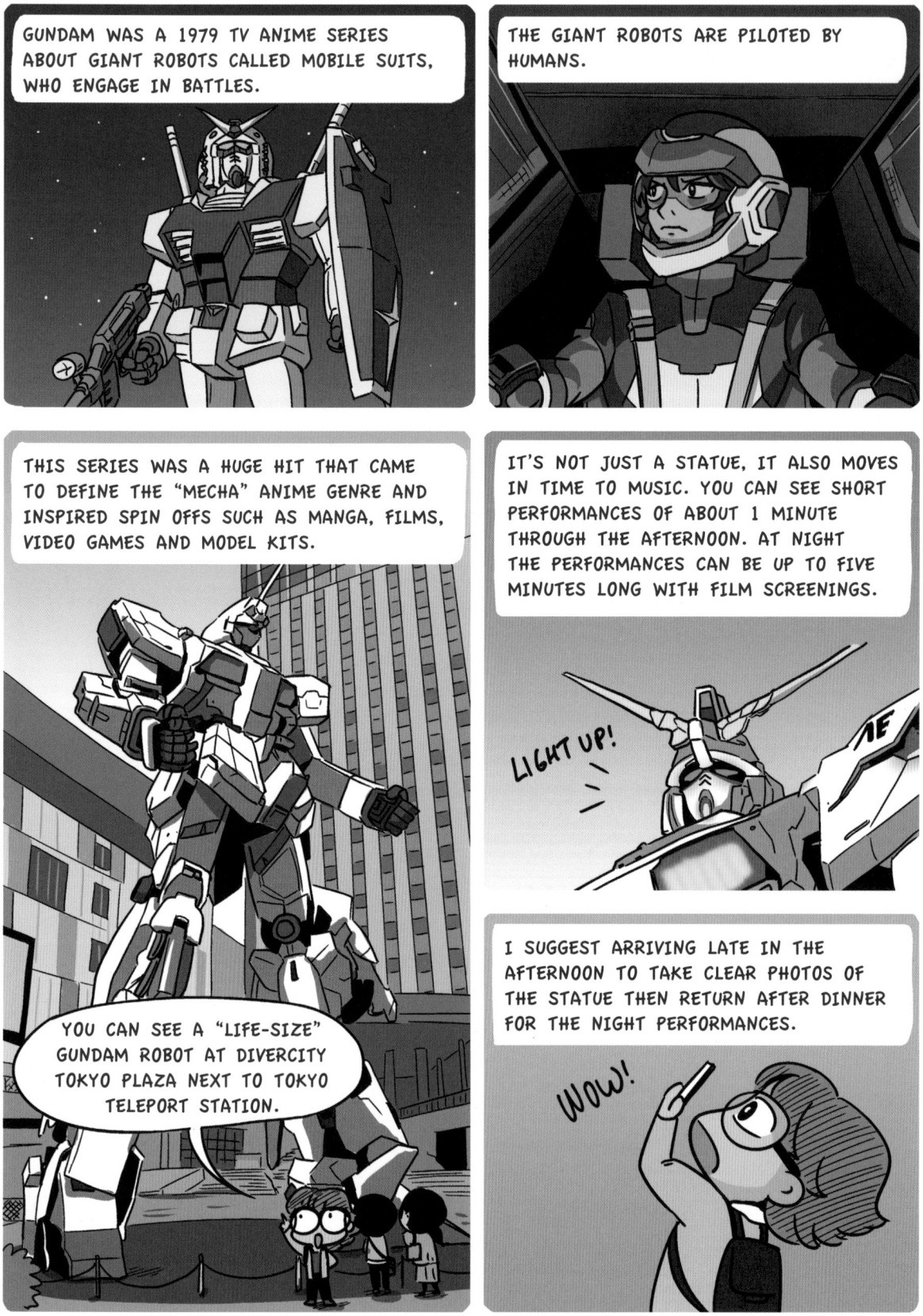

GUNDAM STATUE: unicorn-gundam-statue.jp

NAKANO BROADWAY

I ALREADY MENTIONED ON PAGE 51 THAT MANDARAKE SPECIALIZES IN ALL KINDS OF PRE-OWNED ANIME GOODS.
EACH MANDARAKE SHOP HERE FEATURES A DIFFERENT THEME.
YEAH! THIS ONE SELLS TRADING CARDS...
THAT ONE SELLS ANIME CELS...

THERE ARE OLD COMIC BOOKS AND ART BOOKS THERE.
AREN'T YOU TIRED YET?

THEY EVEN SELL J-POP GOODS!
GOSH, THE CELEBRITIES USED TO LOOK SO YOUNG!

WE CHECKED OUT ALL FOUR LEVELS. WE FOUND THE TAX-FREE COUNTER ON THE TOP FLOOR.
MANDARAKE SERVICE COUNTER
MANDARAKE HAS A CUSTOMER SERVICE CENTER HERE?
LOOKS LIKE YOU CAN DO TAX-FREE SHOPPING AND EVEN MAIL YOUR ITEMS BACK HOME.

TOO BAD I'M JUST LOOKING AND NOT BUYING ANYTHING.
YES, TAKE A LONG LOOK.

I LIKE IT HERE! WE DIDN'T HAVE TO WALK SO MUCH TO SEE EVERYTHING LIKE WE DID IN AKIBA.
YEAH... I GUESS THAT MAKES IT MY PREFERRED CHOICE TOO...

TAKING A MANGA CLASS IN NAKANO

THESE PATTERNS ARE PRINTED ON CLEAR PLASTIC STICKER SHEETS AND STUCK ONTO YOUR DRAWING:

MANGA SCHOOL NAKANO: english.nakanomangaschool.jp

THE GHIBLI MUSEUM

THE GHIBLI MUSEUM IS A MUST-GO FOR PEOPLE WHO LIKE STUDIO GHIBLI ANIMATIONS SUCH AS TOTORO, KIKI'S DELIVERY SERVICE, AND SPIRITED AWAY.

TICKETS MUST BE BOUGHT IN ADVANCE AND CANNOT BE BOUGHT AT THE VENUE. HERE ARE 2 WAYS TO GET YOUR TICKETS:

IF YOU'RE OVERSEAS, YOU CAN BUY ONLINE AT ghibli-museum.jp BUT VERY LIMITED NUMBERS ARE ALLOCATED TO FOREIGNERS.

ASK A FRIEND IN JAPAN TO HELP YOU BUY ONLINE OR FROM A LAWSON CONVENIENCE STORE WITH A LOPPI MACHINE. IT'S BEST TO BUY ONE MONTH IN ADVANCE.

YOU CAN CHOOSE TO ENTER AT 10AM, 12PM, 2PM OR 4PM. REMEMBER TO TELL YOUR FRIEND TO PUT YOUR NAME (SAME AS PASSPORT) ON THE TICKET.

HERE ARE 2 WAYS TO GET TO THE MUSEUM USING THE CHUO LINE FROM SHINJUKU:

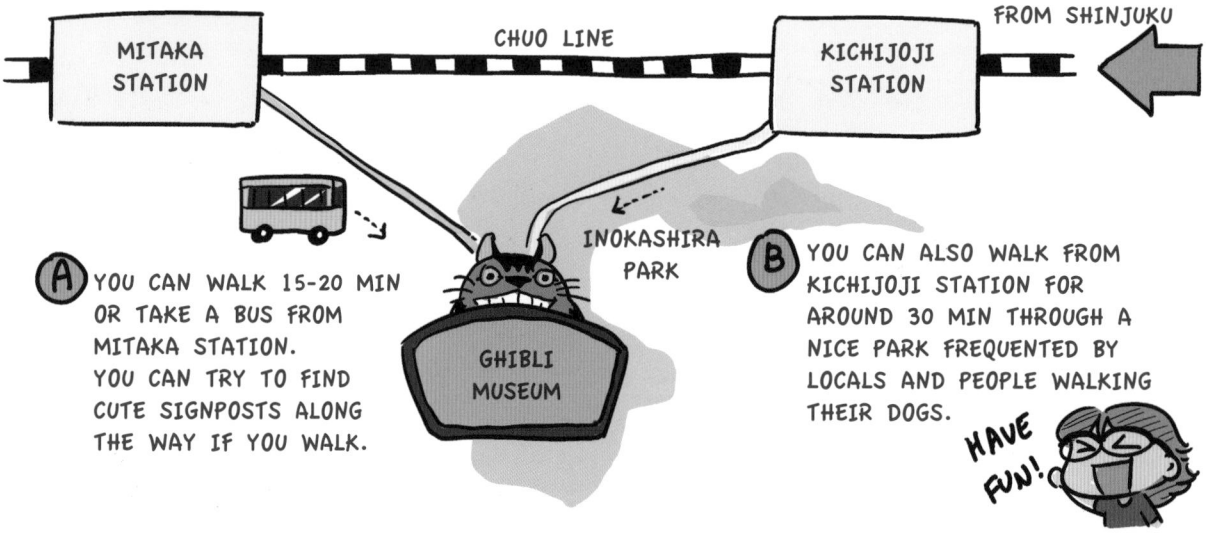

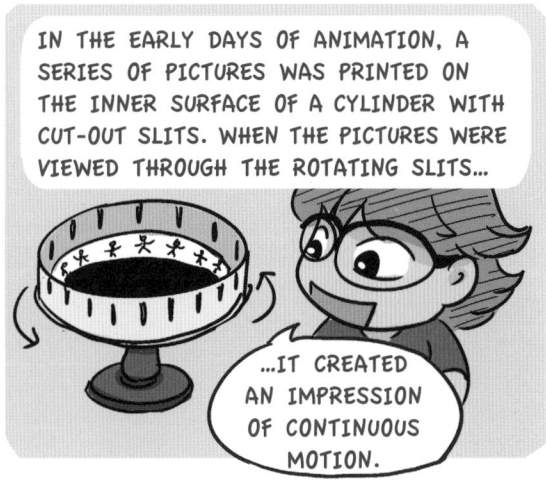

THE MOST IMPRESSIVE ZOETROPE SHOWS TOTORO AND FRIENDS HANGING OUT IN THE PARK.

THE NEXT PERMANENT EXHIBIT IS CALLED "WHERE A FILM IS BORN." IT IS DESIGNED IN SUCH A WAY TO MAKE YOU FEEL AS IF YOU ARE VISITING THE ACTUAL ART STUDIO. THE EXHIBITION IS SPLIT INTO SEVERAL SECTIONS:

1: REFERENCE MATERIALS

2: PREPARATION ROOM

SHELVES FILLED WITH BOOKS, REFERENCE MATERIALS & TOYS

3: PAINTING ROOM

A SLEW OF BRUSHES, PALETTES & PAINT ON THE TABLE AS IF THE ARTIST JUST LEFT THE ROOM

4: STORYBOARD ROOM

5: ANIMATION ROOM

6: CEL COLOR DEPARTMENT

YOU CAN ALSO WATCH THE MUSEUM'S ORIGINAL SHORT ANIMATION AT THEIR THEATER BACK ON THE GROUND FLOOR.

THE ONLY DISAPPOINTMENT WAS THAT NO PHOTOGRAPHY IS ALLOWED INSIDE THE MUSEUM. SO WHATEVER I DREW HERE IS BASED ON MY MEMORY AND HANDWRITTEN NOTES.

SECURITY WAS CONSTANTLY CHECKING ON ME...

THE ONLY DECENT PHOTO SPOT WAS THE ROOFTOP GARDEN WHERE THE ROBOT FROM "CASTLE IN THE SKY" STANDS.

HE IS ALSO SAID TO BE THE GUARDIAN OF THE MUSEUM.

EVEN WHEN YOU EAT AT THEIR CAFE, YOU CAN ONLY TAKE PHOTOS OF YOUR OWN FOOD.

I RECOMMEND ORDERING THE CHOCOLATE CAKE & LATTE BECAUSE THEY HAVE CUTE DRAWINGS ON THEM.

THE PORK CUTLET SANDWICH WAS A BIT TOO CHEWY THOUGH...

MY FIRST VISIT TO GHIBLI WAS IN 2004. AT THAT TIME, THERE WAS NO QUEUE TO GET IN. NOW YOU HAVE TO QUEUE FOR 30 MIN TO EXCHANGE YOUR LAWSON TICKET FOR AN ACTUAL TICKET!

THE ACTUAL TICKET IS A REPRODUCTION OF THE ANIMATION FILM NEGATIVES AND EVERYONE GETS A DIFFERENT DESIGN.

I HAVE COLLECTED 3 SO FAR, AND I HOPE TO COLLECT MORE!

I SPENT A TOTAL OF 4 HOURS HERE BECAUSE OF THE QUEUE TO ENTER THE MUSEUM, AND ANOTHER QUEUE TO ENTER THE CAFE. WITHOUT THE QUEUES, IT WOULD HAVE BEEN JUST 3 HOURS.

MISSION ACCOMPLISHED!

GHIBLI MUSEUM: http://www.ghibli-museum.jp

SANRIO PUROLAND

SANRIO IS THE COMPANY BEHIND YOUR FAVORITE CUTE CHARACTERS SUCH AS HELLO KITTY, MY MELODY, KEROPPI AND MY FAVORITE, GUDETAMA. THEIR WEBSITE IS en.puroland.jp

PUROLAND IS SANRIO'S AMAZING INDOOR AMUSEMENT PARK WHERE YOU CAN MEET THEM IN REAL LIFE!

IT'S LOCATED IN THE WESTERN SUBURBS OF TOKYO:

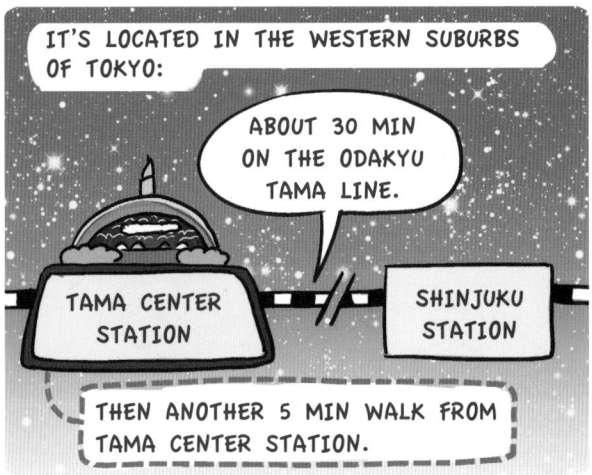

TICKETS CAN BE BOUGHT AT PUROLAND. WEEKDAY TICKETS ARE CHEAPER THAN WEEKEND ONES.

THE PARK CLOSES AT 5PM ON WEEKDAYS SO MY FRIENDS AND I ARRIVED THERE IN THE MORNING TO MAKE SURE WE'D HAVE PLENTY OF TIME.

(WE PURPOSELY TOOK OUR OWN SWEET TIME)

BUT I BOUGHT A FEW THINGS ANYWAY...
ONE FOR MY PENPAL'S BIRTHDAY...
...AND THE OTHER FOR ONE OF MY FANS.

WE GOT HUNGRY AND WENT AROUND LOOKING FOR FOOD.
THE BUFFET DOESN'T LOOK SO SPECIAL.
WE SHOULD TRY SOMETHING INSTAGRAMMABLE.

LET'S TRY THE FOOD COURT!
YEAH, THE FOOD THERE HAS CHARACTER DESIGNS ON IT.
OK!

THE FOOD PROVED TO BE IMPRESSIVE.
WOW MINT GREEN AND PINK COLORED CURRY!
BUT SEEMS ARTIFICIALLY COLORED?

I ENDED UP ORDERING A WESTERN-STYLE MEAL, WITH A MIFFY CAKE AND COOKIE.
THEY WERE VERY CUTE AND TASTED ALRIGHT.

AFTER LUNCH, WE TRIED TO LOOK FOR RIDES. BUT THERE WAS ONLY ONE, A BOAT RIDE, AND THAT WAS CLOSED.
IS IT BECAUSE IT'S A WEEKDAY?
I DON'T KNOW.

NEVERTHELESS, WE HAD FUN PLAYING VIRTUAL REALITY GAMES SUCH AS THE ONE THAT MAPS AN ELABORATELY CUTE DRESS ON YOU.

SANRIO PUROLAND: https://en.puroland.jp

THE DORAEMON MUSEUM

FOR THOSE WHO ARE NOT FAMILIAR WITH THIS MANGA AND ANIME, IT IS THE STORY OF A ROBOT CAT NAMED "DORAEMON" FROM THE FUTURE, WHO GOES BACK IN TIME TO HELP A BOY CALLED NOBITA.

THE OFFICIAL NAME OF THE MUSEUM IS THE FUJIKO F FUJIO MUSEUM, NAMED AFTER THE ARTIST. IT IS LOCATED IN THE WESTERN SUBURBS OF TOKYO. THE WEBSITE IS fujiko-museum.com/english/

A 35 MIN TRAIN RIDE FROM SHINJUKU ON THE ODAKYU LINE.

NOBORITO STATION

SHINJUKU STATION

MUKOGAOKAYUEN STATION

DORAEMON MUSEUM

A

YOU CAN TAKE A SHUTTLE BUS FROM NOBORITO STATION THAT WILL COST 210 YEN AND TAKES AROUND 10 MIN.

B

YOU CAN ALSO CHOOSE TO WALK FOR AROUND 16 MIN FROM MUKOGAOKAYUEN STATION. THERE ARE MANY CUTE STATUES ALONG THE CANAL ON THE OPPOSITE SIDE.

TICKETS MUST BE BOUGHT IN ADVANCE FROM LOPPI MACHINES AT LAWSON CONVENIENCE STORES. YOU DON'T HAVE TO BUY THEM A MONTH AHEAD LIKE YOU DO FOR GHIBLI, BUT IT'S BETTER TO BUY THEM A FEW DAYS BEFORE YOUR VISIT. YOU CAN CHOOSE TO ENTER AT 10AM, 12PM, 2PM OR 4PM.

WE TOOK THE SHUTTLE BUS FROM NOBORITO STATION.
EVEN THE CARD READER IS SPECIALLY DESIGNED!

WHEN YOU REACH THE MUSEUM, YOU'LL BE GREETED BY A CONCIERGE. YOU CAN BORROW AUDIO GUIDES IN ENGLISH, CHINESE OR KOREAN.

THERE ARE ORIGINAL DRAWINGS ON DISPLAY AND MANY HAVE TURNED YELLOW WITH AGE. YOU CAN SEE THE CORRECTION FLUID MARKS MADE BY THE ARTIST.
TOO BAD, NO PHOTOS ALLOWED.

THERE ARE ALSO CUSTOM-MADE WALL SHELVES FILLED WITH HAND-DRAWN ANIMATION PAPERS.
THEY ARE ALL SEALED BEHIND THIS HUGE GLASS WALL.

THE COOLEST PART OF THE EXHIBIT IS THE PROJECTION MAPPING, SHOWING HOW THE MANGA WERE MADE.

THE LAST PART OF THE EXHIBIT IS AN ORIGINAL SHORT FILM AT THE MUSEUM THEATER. BUT NO TRANSLATION IS AVAILABLE FROM THE AUDIO GUIDE.
I WILL TRY MY BEST TO TRANSLATE...

OUTSIDE THERE ARE MORE EXHIBITS WHERE YOU CAN HAVE FUN DOING WEIRD POSES...

THERE IS ALSO A SMALL GIFT SHOP SELLING SWEET SNACKS...

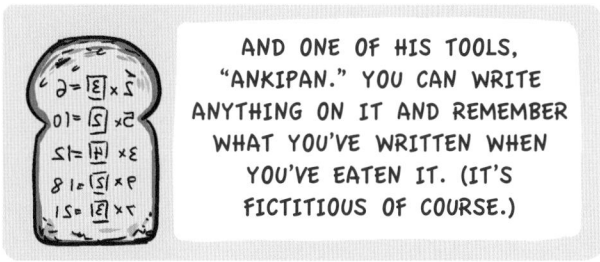

FOR OUR RETURN TRIP, WE DECIDE TO WALK TO MUKOGAOKAYUEN STATION TO TAKE PHOTOS OF THE CUTE STATUES AND SIGNPOSTS ALONG THE WAY.

DORAEMON MUSEUM: fujiko-museum.com/english/

CHAPTER 3

ADVENTURES IN JAPANESE FOOD

JAPANESE SET MEALS ARE CALLED "TEISHOKU" AND OFTEN CONSIST OF THE FOLLOWING:

SET MEALS ARE OFTEN SERVED IN SMALL BOWLS OR PLATES PLACED IN A TRAY. THEY CAN ALSO BE PUT TOGETHER IN A BENTO.

* THIS MEANS "BON APPETIT" IN JAPANESE

JAPANESE NOODLES

RAMEN

TOPPED WITH A PIECE OF SEAWEED, PORK, SLICED BAMBOO SHOOT AND A SOFT-BOILED EGG.

POPULAR RAMEN CHAIN RESTAURANTS ARE ICHIRAN, IPPUDO AND MUTEKIYA.

USUALLY SERVED WITH BROTH. THE MOST POPULAR FLAVORS ARE:

SHOYU	SHIO	MISO	TONKOTSU
SOY SAUCE	SALT	FERMENTED SOYBEANS	PORK BONES

HOW TO EAT TSUKEMEN

TSUKEMEN IS A KIND OF RAMEN WITH THE NOODLES SEPARATED FROM THE BROTH, WHICH IS MORE CONCENTRATED THAN REGULAR SOUP.

FIRST, PICK UP SOME NOODLES AND DIP THEM INTO THE BROTH.

AFTER YOU FINISH ALL THE NOODLES, POUR HOT WATER INTO THE BROTH AND DRINK IT AS A SOUP.

UDON

THE BROTH IS PLAINER THAN RAMEN BROTH. SERVED WITH JUST NOODLES OR TOPPED WITH SCALLIONS.

I RECOMMEND MARUGAME SEIMEN, A CHAIN STORE THAT SERVES AFFORDABLE AND DELICIOUS UDON.

BECAUSE UDON ABSORBS THE FLAVORS OF THE BROTH AND OTHER INGREDIENTS, IT COMES IN MANY DIFFERENT VARIETIES LIKE CURRY UDON AND STIR-FRIED UDON, ALSO CALLED YAKI-UDON.

CURRY GRAVY WITH MEAT AND VEGGIES IS POURED OVER THE NOODLES

CURRY UDON

MEAT AND VEGETABLES ARE ADDED AND THE NOODLES ARE STIR-FRIED.

YAKI-UDON

HOW TO ORDER AT MARUGAME SEIMEN

AT THE COUNTER, ORDER THE KIND OF UDON YOU WANT FIRST, THEN TAKE ANOTHER EMPTY PLATE IF YOU WANT TO ADD TEMPURA.

TAKE THE TEMPURA YOU WANT AND PAY AT THE END OF THE LINE.

SOBA

COLD SOBA

SOBA SERVED CHILLED ON A BAMBOO TRAY IS POPULAR DURING SUMMER. BUT YOU CAN ALSO ORDER IT IN A HOT SOUP.

SOBA IN HOT SOUP

YAKISOBA

STIR-FRIED SOBA WITH MEAT AND VEGETABLES

HOW TO EAT COLD SOBA

MIX THE WASABI AND GRATED SPRING ONIONS INTO THE DIPPING SAUCE.

DIP YOUR SOBA INTO SAUCE AND EAT THEM FROM THE CUP.

THE WAITER WILL GIVE YOU A POT OF HOT SOBAYU TO POUR INTO YOUR LEFTOVER TSUYU TO DRINK.

SOMEN

SOMEN IS ALSO USUALLY SERVED COLD AND IS POPULAR DURING SUMMER. LIKE COLD SOBA, YOU DIP THE NOODLES INTO THE TSUYU AND EAT THEM FROM THE CUP.

HOW TO EAT NAGASHI SOMEN

NAGASHI SOMEN MEANS FLOWING NOODLES. IT REQUIRES SETTING UP LONG OPEN BAMBOO STEMS WITH FLOWING COLD WATER AND PLACING SMALL BUNDLES OF SOMEN UPSTREAM. UNFORTUNATELY BECAUSE OF THE COMPLICATED SETUP, IT IS ONLY DONE DURING FESTIVALS. THERE ARE A FEW RESTAURANTS SELLING SOMEN IN TOKYO BUT WITHOUT THIS SETUP.

SUSHI

I REALLY LOVE TO EAT SUSHI AND THE MOST POPULAR KIND WITH TOURISTS IS THE CONVEYOR-BELT STYLE SUSHI CALLED "KAITEN SUSHI."

THE CHEF WILL STAND IN THE MIDDLE SO YOU CAN ORDER YOUR SUSHI DIRECTLY FROM HIM AND HE WILL MAKE IT ON THE SPOT FOR YOU.

ALTERNATIVELY, YOU CAN JUST GRAB A PRE-PREPARED SUSHI PLATE GOING AROUND ON THE CONVEYOR BELT.

THE COLOR OF THE PLATES REPRESENTS THE DIFFERENT PRICES YOU HAVE TO PAY. SO IF YOU'RE ON TIGHT BUDGET, YOU CAN GO FOR THE CHEAPEST COLOR.

130 YEN

160 YEN

220 YEN

360 YEN

THEY ALSO HAVE FREE-FLOW GREEN TEA. JUST TAKE THE CUP ON THE TABLE, PUT IN SOME GREEN TEA POWDER OR A TEA BAG, THEN PRESS THE TAP TO DISPENSE HOT WATER.

WHEN YOU'RE DONE, ASK THE WAITER FOR THE BILL. HE WILL COUNT THE EMPTY PLATES YOU HAVE AND RECORD THEM ON A SLIP OF PAPER. TAKE THAT PAPER TO PAY AT THE CASHIER.

OKAIKEI ONEGAISHIMASU!

CROSSING OF INDEX FINGERS MEANS BILL PLEASE.

YES!

A KAITEN SUSHI RESTAURANT I LIKE IS HEIROKU SUSHI (heiroku.jp)
MY FRIEND LIKES TENKA SUSHI (tenkazushi.co.jp) IN IKEBUKURO.

YOU CAN ALSO FIND MANY SUSHI RESTAURANTS AT TSUKIJI FISH MARKET. A NICE AND AFFORDABLE ONE IS SUSHI-ZANMAI. THEIR MAIN BRANCH IS HUGE AND OPEN 24 HOURS, EVEN DURING NEW YEAR.
すしざんまい
SUSHI ZANMAI
BUT IT'S NOT KAITEN SUSHI STYLE.

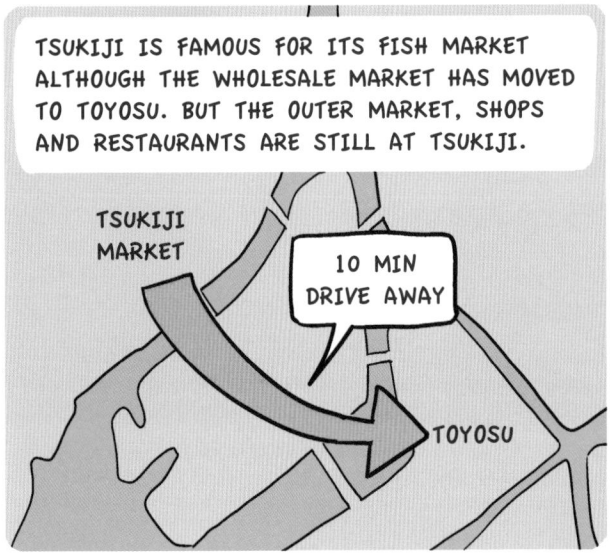
TSUKIJI IS FAMOUS FOR ITS FISH MARKET ALTHOUGH THE WHOLESALE MARKET HAS MOVED TO TOYOSU. BUT THE OUTER MARKET, SHOPS AND RESTAURANTS ARE STILL AT TSUKIJI.
TSUKIJI MARKET
10 MIN DRIVE AWAY
TOYOSU

THE WHOLESALE MARKET IS ONLY FOR FISH DEALERS...
AND MANY SHOPS AND SUSHI RESTAURANTS ARE STILL AT THE OLD OUTER MARKET.

BESIDES SUSHI-ZANMAI, MY FRIENDS RECOMMEND OTHER POPULAR SUSHI CHAIN RESTAURANTS IN TOKYO.
"KURA SUSHI" (kura-corpo.co.jp) HAS A GREAT GASHAPON CONCEPT.
"SUSHI NO MIDORI" (sushinomidori.co.jp) IS NICE TOO.

BUT IF YOU HAVE 20,000 YEN OR MORE TO SPEND, YOU CAN TRY ONE OF THE PREMIUM SUSHI RESTAURANTS IN GINZA.
I DON'T KNOW WHAT JIRO'S SUSHI TASTES LIKE BUT I'M HAPPY WITH THE SUSHI AT GINZA SUSHIKOH.

HERE ARE THE SPECIAL NAMES YOU CAN USE WHEN DINING AT A SUSHI RESTAURANT (THEY CAN ONLY BE USED THERE):

TYPES OF SUSHI

SUSHI NAMES

MAGURO
TUNA

CHUTORO
SEMI-FATTY TUNA

OTORO
FATTY TUNA

NEGITORO
MIXED FATTY TUNA AND SPRING ONION

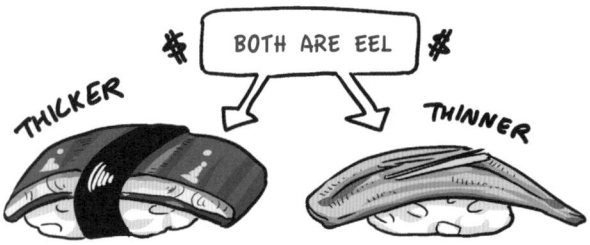

UNAGI
FRESHWATER EEL

ANAGO
SEA EEL

UNI
SEA URCHIN

SAKE/ SA-MON
SALMON

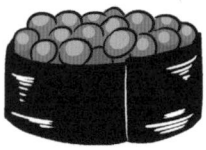

IKURA
SALMON ROE

IKA
SQUID

EBI
PRAWN

TSUNAMAYO
TUNA MAYONNAISE

YAKITORI

MY FAVORITE YAKITORI PLACE IS HACHIMAN

HACHIMAN WEBSITE: yakitori-hachiman.com

SUKIYAKI AND SHABU-SHABU

THE MEAT IS SIMMERED WITH A SWEET SAUCE IN A SHALLOW POT.

THE MEAT IS BOILED IN A SOUP, SOMETIMES WITH 2 DIFFERENT SOUP BASES.

CRACK THE RAW EGG INTO THE SMALL BOWL PROVIDED AND MIX IT WITH YOUR CHOPSTICKS. THEN DIP THE COOKED MEAT INTO THE RAW EGG TO EAT. IF YOU DON'T LIKE RAW EGG, YOU CAN COOK IT IN THE HOT POT.

THERE ARE DIFFERENT KINDS OF DIPPING SAUCES LIKE SOY SAUCE, CITRUS AND SESAME. YOU CAN EVEN MIX THEM TOGETHER TO MAKE YOUR OWN UNIQUE SAUCE!

OTHER JAPANESE DISHES

GYUDON
BEEF RICE BOWL

KATSUDON
PORK CUTLET RICE BOWL

OYAKODON
CHICKEN & EGG RICE BOWL

KAISENDON
SEAFOOD RICE BOWL

TENDON
TEMPURA RICE BOWL

BUTADON
PORK RICE BOWL

UNADON
EEL RICE BOWL

CHIRASHIDON
CHOPPED SEAFOOD & VEGETABLE RICE BOWL

OTHER FOODS

TEMPURA
BATTERED & FRIED SEAFOOD AND VEGETABLES

KUSHIKATSU
FRIED SKEWERED MEAT & VEGETABLES

TAKOYAKI
OCTOPUS BALLS

TAMAGOYAKI
ROLLED OMELETTE

GYOZA
CRISPY DUMPLINGS

ODEN
SIMMERED HOT POT

CHAWANMUSHI
EGG CUSTARD WITH SHRIMP, MUSHROOMS, ETC

NATTO
FERMENTED SOYBEANS

EATING ON A BUDGET

THERE ARE 3 MAJOR GYUDON CHAIN RESTAURANTS IN JAPAN, ALL OF WHICH SERVE GYUDON FOR 500 YEN:

SUKIYA

MATSUYA

YOSHINOYA

BESIDES GYUDON, THEY ALSO SERVE OTHER SIDE DISHES AND SEASONAL FOODS BUT YOUR MEAL WILL BE OVER 500 YEN IF YOU ORDER THEM.

SALAD

TONJIRU
(A KIND OF PORK SOUP)

COLD TOFU

EGG

YOU CAN ALSO ADD A BIT OF PICKLED GINGER TO EAT WITH THE BEEF.

THOUGH ITALIANS SHOULD PROBABLY JUST AVOID THIS.

TRADITIONAL JAPANESE DESSERTS

TRADITIONAL JAPANESE SWEETS, CALLED "WAGASHI," ARE TYPICALLY FILLED WITH SWEET RED BEAN PASTE.

SMOOTH TEXTURED PASTE IS CALLED "KOSHIAN."

CHUNKY TEXTURED PASTE IS CALLED "TSUBUAN."

I ALSO LOVE MATCHA FLAVORED SWEET SNACKS LIKE ICE-CREAM, COOKIES AND CAKES.

* MATCHA IS FINELY POWDERED GREEN TEA.

HERE ARE SOME COMMON WAGASHI SWEETS. BASEMENT FOOD HALLS IN DEPARTMENT STORES USUALLY HAVE A GOOD SELECTION AND SOMETIMES SAMPLES YOU CAN TRY.

DANGO
SMALL AND CHEWY, MADE FROM RICE FLOUR. TYPICALLY SERVED WITH A SWEET SAUCE OR RED BEAN PASTE.

TAIYAKI
CRISPY THIN PANCAKES IN A FISH SHAPE FILLED WITH SWEET BEAN PASTE OR OTHER FILLINGS LIKE CHOCOLATE OR CHEESE.

MANJU
BAKED AND FILLED WITH BEAN PASTE OR OTHER SWEET FILLINGS.

DORAYAKI
ROUND PANCAKES FILLED WITH BEAN PASTE OR OTHER FILLINGS LIKE MATCHA.

DAIFUKU
SOFT RICE CAKES FILLED WITH RED BEAN PASTE OR OTHER SWEET FILLINGS.

NAMAGASHI
CAKES MADE FROM RICE FLOUR, FILLED WITH RED BEAN PASTE AND INTRICATELY SHAPED.

YOKAN
SWEET AND FIRM JELLY-LIKE SWEETS MADE FROM RED BEAN PASTE, AGAR AND SUGAR.

JAPANESE DRINKS

IT'S GOOD TO KNOW THE JAPANESE NAMES WHEN ORDERING YOUR DRINKS. MANY OF THEM ARE BASED ON ENGLISH, BUT WITH A DIFFERENT PRONUNCIATION.

NON-ALCOHOLIC

MATCHA LATTE
FINE GREEN TEA LATTE

O-CHA
JAPANESE GREEN TEA

URON-CHA
CHINESE TEA (OOLONG TEA)

KO-RA
COLA

OMIZU/OHIYA
WATER/COLD WATER

OYU
HOT WATER

KO-HI
COFFEE

KO-CHA
ENGLISH TEA

ALCOHOLIC

BI-RU
BEER

KASHISU ORENJI
CASSIS ORANGE

UMESHU ROKKU
PLUM WINE ON THE ROCKS

UMESHU SODA
PLUM WINE WITH SODA

YUZU SOUR/ YUZU CHUHAI
CITRUS+SHOCHU+SODA

LEMON SOUR/ LEMON CHUHAI
LEMON+SHOCHU+SODA

SAKE/O-SAKE
SAKE

ABOUT SAKE AND SHOCHU

BUT THERE IS A SAYING:

WARM = FOR CHEAPER SAKE...

CHILLED = FOR EXPENSIVE SAKE...

CHAPTER 4

SHOPPING HEAVEN

LARGE STORES, RESTAURANTS AND CONVENIENCE STORES ACCEPT CREDIT CARDS NOW, AND SOME ARE BEGINNING TO ACCEPT MOBILE PAYMENTS LIKE APPLE PAY OR ALIPAY. BUT CASH IS STILL KING IN JAPAN. BE SURE TO ALWAYS CARRY ENOUGH CASH WITH YOU, ESPECIALLY OUTSIDE THE MAJOR CITIES. YOU CAN WITHDRAW CASH FROM YOUR CREDIT CARD AT ATM MACHINES IN SOME CONVENIENCE STORES LIKE 7-ELEVEN AND LAWSON.

TAX-FREE SHOPPING

IT IS NOW VERY EASY TO GET A TAX REFUND IN JAPAN. FIRST, LOOK FOR THIS TAX-FREE LOGO:

GOODS ARE DIVIDED INTO 2 CATEGORIES:

YOU MUST SPEND MORE THAN 5,000 YEN IN EACH CATEGORY TO GET A TAX REFUND, AND YOU CAN'T COMBINE GOODS FROM DIFFERENT CATEGORIES. IN ART SHOPS, PAPER AND NOTEPADS ARE CLASSIFIED AS CONSUMABLES.

TO SHOP TAX FREE, FIRST, YOU HAVE TO TELL THE CASHIER WHEN MAKING YOUR PAYMENT THAT YOU WANT TO APPLY FOR TAX FREE. SHE WILL THEN SEPARATE YOUR PURCHASES INTO THE 2 CATEGORIES.

PAY THE FULL PRICE FIRST, THEN GO TO THE TAX-FREE COUNTER TO FILL OUT THE FORMS AND COLLECT YOUR REFUND.

YOU'RE NOT SUPPOSED TO OPEN THE SEALED BAG BEFORE YOU LEAVE JAPAN BUT MOST TOURISTS DON'T CARE BECAUSE IT'S CUMBERSOME TO PACK INTO YOUR LUGGAGE WHILE SEALED. JUST REMEMBER TO PASS YOUR PASSPORT TO

CUSTOMS DURING DEPARTURE. THEY WILL REMOVE THE RECEIPTS. YOU'RE SUPPOSED TO SHOW THEM THE SEALED BAGS BUT THEY RARELY ASK. IF THEY DO, JUST SAY THEY'RE IN YOUR CHECKED LUGGAGE.

SHOPPING FOR SOUVENIRS

THE SECOND SHOP I WOULD LIKE TO RECOMMEND IS LOFT.

Loft

loft.co.jp

LOFT HAS A SIMILAR CONCEPT TO TOKYU HANDS, SELLING CREATIVE LIFESTYLE GOODS.

MUJI IS ANOTHER LIFESTYLE STORE SELLING THEIR OWN HOUSE BRAND OF NON-BRANDED MINIMALIST PRODUCTS.

MUJI
無印良品

muji.net

IF YOU'RE ON A BUDGET, I RECOMMEND DON QUIJOTE ("DONKI" FOR SHORT), WHICH I BRIEFLY TALKED ABOUT ON PAGE 51. IT'S A JAPANESE DISCOUNT SHOP SELLING ALMOST ANYTHING! THEY ALSO HAVE BRANCHES ALL OVER JAPAN. THE WEBSITE IS donki.com

IT'S A GREAT PLACE TO BUY INTERESTING JAPANESE SNACKS, INCLUDING KIT KATS WITH A HUGE VARIETY OF FLAVORS NOT AVAILABLE ANYWHERE ELSE!

IF YOU LIKE TOYS, YOU SHOULD CHECK OUT HAKUHINKAN TOY PARK IN GINZA.
THEY ALSO HAVE BRANCHES AT THE AIRPORTS BUT THIS PLACE IS MUCH BIGGER.
博品館
HAKUHINKAN
TOY PARK
hakuhinkan.co.jp

UNLIKE THE ANIME-RELATED TOY SHOPS IN AKIHABARA, THEY HAVE MORE OF YOUR REGULAR TOYS.

LAST BUT NOT LEAST, YOU CAN DO LAST-MINUTE SHOPPING AT THE DUTY FREE SHOPS AT THE AIRPORTS.
TAX FREE AKIHABARA
NARITA HAS MORE SHOPS THAN HANEDA AND AN ELECTRONICS SECTION TOO.

THE MOST POPULAR GIFT ITEMS ARE SNACKS:
KIT KAT
POTATO FARM FRENCH FRIES
TOKYO BANANA
SHIROI KOIBITO

OF COURSE, YOU CAN ALSO BUY JAPANESE SAKE OR SHOCHU HERE TOO.
日本酒

IF YOU'RE SICK OF MAINSTREAM SNACKS, I RECOMMEND BUYING GALBO. IT IS A CHOCOLATE BISCUIT SNACK COATED WITH FLAVORS LIKE GREEN TEA, STRAWBERRY OR WHITE CHOCOLATE.
galbo mini
galbo mini
galbo mini
galbo mini
YOU CAN BUY THEM FROM ANY CONVENIENCE STORE, ENJOY!

THE UBIQUITOUS 100 YEN SHOPS

AWESOME ELECTRONICS

HERE ARE SOME WORTHWHILE ELECTRONICS TO CONSIDER TAKING HOME:

① RICE COOKER.

SERIOUSLY, THE RANGE AND QUALITY OF RICE COOKERS IN JAPAN IS AMAZING AND PRICES ARE VERY GOOD. MANY HAVE MULTIPLE FUNCTIONS LIKE MAKING SOUP TOO. JUST MAKE SURE THEY WILL WORK WITH YOUR ELECTRICAL POWER AT HOME. (ASK THE SHOP STAFF.)

② CAMERA LENSES AND OTHER CAMERA EQUIPMENT THAT IS MADE IN JAPAN.

③ AN ELECTRONIC DICTIONARY IF YOU'RE LEARNING JAPANESE.

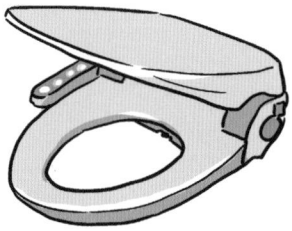

④ AMAZING TOILET SEATS... HEATED IN WINTER AND WITH A BUTT-WASHING FUNCTION TOO.

COSMETICS AND BEAUTY PRODUCTS

CONVENIENCE STORES

THERE ARE MANY CONVENIENCE STORE CHAINS IN JAPAN AND THEY ALL OPERATE 24 HR!

THEY ARE CALLED "CONBINI" FOR SHORT.

THEY SELL MANY THINGS FROM DAILY GOODS TO FOOD SUCH AS SANDWICHES, BENTO BOXES, SNACKS AND BREAD. SOME EVEN SELL FRESH PRODUCE SUCH AS MEAT, FRUIT AND VEGETABLES.

THEY ALSO SELL THE COMMON CLEAR PLASTIC UMBRELLAS THAT EVERYONE SEEMS TO USE WHEN IT'S RAINING.

THE MAJOR CONVENIENCE STORES ARE 7-ELEVEN, FAMILY MART AND LAWSON.

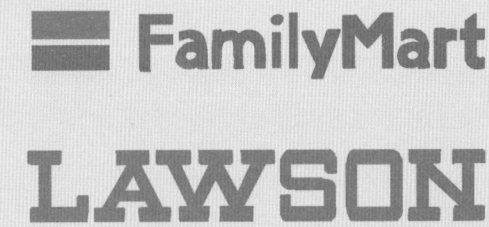

I LIKE FAMILY MART FOR THEIR TASTY FRIED CHICKEN CALLED "FAMICHIKI," WHICH MAKES A GREAT SNACK WHEN YOU'RE A LITTLE BIT HUNGRY.

LAWSON ALSO HAVE GOOD CHICKEN NUGGETS CALLED "KARAAGEKUN" THAT COME IN DIFFERENT FLAVORS!

FOR BREAD, I LIKE THE CHEWY KIND CALLED "MOCHIMOCHI" OR "MOCHI," SOLD AT ALL THE CONVENIENCE STORES.

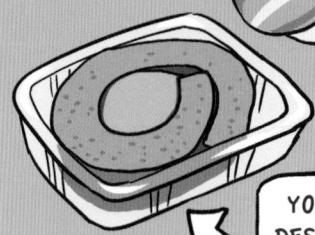

YOU CAN BUY NICE DESSERTS AT ALL OF THEM (THOUGH MY FAVORITE IS FAMILY MART).

IF YOU WANT TO BUY FRESH FRUIT AND VEGETABLES BUT CAN'T FIND A SUPERMARKET, LOOK FOR A LAWSON STORE 100.
LIKE 100 YEN SHOPS, ALMOST EVERYTHING IS PRICED AT 100 YEN, AS THEY TARGET BUDGET-CONSCIOUS CUSTOMERS.
LAWSON STORE 100
酒

NATURAL LAWSON
LAWSON ALSO HAS AN UPSCALE BRAND CALLED "NATURAL LAWSON" THAT SELLS HEALTHIER AND AND NICELY PACKAGED SNACKS AND FOOD.
NATURAL LAWSON

THERE ARE SO MANY CONVENIENCE STORES IN JAPAN VYING FOR BUSINESS, SO FOOD AND DRINK LINES ARE CONSTANTLY BEING REFRESHED TO ENTICE CUSTOMERS TO RETURN TO TRY NEW FLAVORS.
SO YOU MIGHT FIND CHERRY BLOSSOM-FLAVOR CAKES AND BREAD DURING SPRING...
PUMPKIN AND CHESTNUT BREAD AND TARTS DURING FALL.

IN WINTER, MOST CONVENIENCE STORES WILL ALSO SERVE ODEN, A KIND OF HOT POT WITH DIFFERENT INGREDIENTS SIMMERED IN A SOY SAUCE BROTH.

THE ONLY ODD THING ABOUT CONVENIENCE STORES IS THE SALE OF SOFT PORN MAGAZINES, OFTEN BLATANTLY NEAR THE ENTRANCE OR NEXT TO THE COMICS AND FASHION MAGAZINES.

SO IF YOU HAVE KIDS, YOU MIGHT WANT TO STEER THEM AWAY FROM THIS SECTION.

THIS SERVICE IS CALLED TA-Q-BIN AND IS OFFERED BY A LOGISTICS COMPANY WORKING WITH CONVENIENCE STORES.

TOKYO'S MAIN SHOPPING DISTRICTS

HERE IS MY CONCISE INTRODUCTION TO THE DIFFERENT SHOPPING DISTRICTS IN TOKYO:

HARAJUKU

FOR TEENS LOOKING FOR CHEAP AND GOTHIC CLOTHES. YOU CAN FIND MANY PRE-LOVED VINTAGE ITEMS TOO.

SHINJUKU

PRETTY MUCH FOR ANYBODY UNLESS YOU ARE LOOKING FOR GOTHIC OR LOLITA. IT'S GREAT FOR SHOES!

SHIBUYA

FOR YOUNG WORKING ADULTS. THE ICONIC SHIBUYA 109 BUILDING HAS MANY TRENDY CLOTHING SHOPS AND THE AREA IS FULL OF OTHER SHOPS AND BRANDS.

UENO & ASAKUSA

NOT MANY SHOPS SELLING CLOTHES OTHER THAN THE DEPARTMENT STORES. ASAKUSA HAS LOTS OF SHOPS SELLING TRADITIONAL ITEMS THAT MAKE PERFECT SOUVENIRS.

OMOTESANDO & AOYAMA

THE DESIGNER CLOTHES HERE ARE A BIT AVANT-GARDE AND VERY PRICEY. I ONLY WINDOW SHOP HERE.

GINZA

WITH THE EXCEPTION OF MY BELOVED UNIQLO, THIS DISTRICT IS FOR THE RICH. YOU'LL FIND MANY LUXURY BRANDS HERE.

BUYING KAWAII CLOTHES

OH, IF YOU'RE LOOKING FOR BURBERRY ITEMS EXCLUSIVE TO THE JAPANESE MARKET, THEY ARE NOW UNDER THE BLUE LABEL CRESTBRIDGE BRAND BECAUSE OF LICENSING ISSUES WITH BURBERRY.

BLUE LABEL
CRESTBRIDGE

crestbridge.jp

IF YOU'RE ON A BUDGET, TRY UNIQLO. THEIR CLOTHES ARE GOOD QUALITY AND CHEAPER IN JAPAN THAN OVERSEAS (uniqlo.com/jp).
THEIR BIGGEST BRANCH IS IN GINZA WITH 12 FLOORS.

HEATTECH IS ONE OF THEIR MOST POPULAR LINES, RETAINING BODY HEAT VERY WELL DURING WINTER.

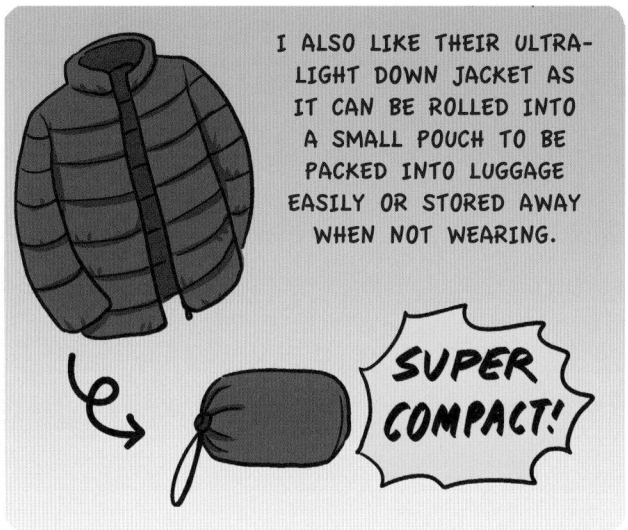
I ALSO LIKE THEIR ULTRA-LIGHT DOWN JACKET AS IT CAN BE ROLLED INTO A SMALL POUCH TO BE PACKED INTO LUGGAGE EASILY OR STORED AWAY WHEN NOT WEARING.
SUPER COMPACT!

THEIR "ROOM WEAR" LINE AND WIRELESS BRAS ARE ALSO VERY COMFORTABLE.
UNIQLO ROOM WEAR KEEPS ME COMFY AT HOME ALL YEAR ROUND!

BUT OF COURSE AT THIS AFFORDABLE PRICE YOU GET GOOD QUALITY BUT NOT MUCH BEAUTY OR FASHION.
THERE'S A JOKE THAT YOU WEAR UNIQLO UNDERWEAR IF YOU ARE SINGLE WITH NO PARTNER TO IMPRESS...

IF YOU WANT EVEN CHEAPER PRICES, UNIQLO HAS A SISTER BRAND CALLED "GU" FOR TEENS.
THE QUALITY IS NOT AS GOOD AS UNIQLO BUT SOME PEOPLE DON'T MIND BECAUSE IT'S SUPER CHEAP.
GU
GUGU

tutuanna*
PINK LABEL
FOR SOCKS AND CUTE STOCKINGS, I LIKE TUTUANNA (tutanna.com).

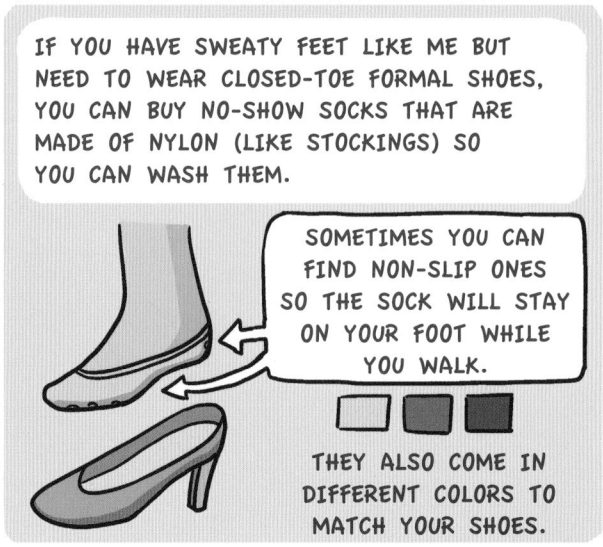
IF YOU HAVE SWEATY FEET LIKE ME BUT NEED TO WEAR CLOSED-TOE FORMAL SHOES, YOU CAN BUY NO-SHOW SOCKS THAT ARE MADE OF NYLON (LIKE STOCKINGS) SO YOU CAN WASH THEM.
SOMETIMES YOU CAN FIND NON-SLIP ONES SO THE SOCK WILL STAY ON YOUR FOOT WHILE YOU WALK.
THEY ALSO COME IN DIFFERENT COLORS TO MATCH YOUR SHOES.

FOR SHOES, ABC MART (abc-mart.co.jp) HAVE A GOOD SELECTION AND HAVE STORES ALL OVER TOKYO.
BUT THEY'RE NOT TAX FREE AND I DON'T FIND THE DESIGNS TRENDY ENOUGH.
ABC-MART
SALE
HOWEVER YOU CAN STILL BUY GOOD INSOLES FOR YOUR SHOES HERE.

PLAZA
I PREFER SHOE PLAZA IF YOU WANT TO LOOK FOR FASHIONABLE SPORTS SHOES (chiyodagrp.co.jp).
AND THEY'RE TAX FREE TOO!

DEPARTMENT STORES, SUCH AS KEIO AND ODAKYU IN SHINJUKU, ALSO OFFER VERY ATTRACTIVE DESIGNS.
BUT PRICES ARE A BIT HIGHER.

BESIDES SHOES, I BUY TRANSPARENT STICK-ON PADDING FOR MY HEELED SANDALS TO CUSHION MY FEET.
LIKE THIS ONE THAT CUSHIONS THE BALL OF YOUR FOOT AND PREVENTS YOUR TOES FROM SLIPPING THROUGH AT THE SAME TIME.

BOOKS AND MAGAZINES

tsutaya.tsite.jp

THE GINZA AND ROPPONGI BRANCHES FOCUS ON ART BOOKS AND SOUVENIRS, AND ARE SMALLER THAN THE DAIKANYAMA BRANCH.

IF YOU ARE MORE INTO BOOKS THAN SIPPING COFFEE, TRY KINOKUNIYA OR BOOK 1ST.
THEY BOTH HAVE BRANCHES IN SHINJUKU. KINOKUNIYA IS NEAR ISETAN DEPT. STORE AND BOOK 1ST IS IN COCOON TOWER.

THEY HAVE A GOOD SELECTION OF JAPANESE AND WESTERN BOOKS.
BOOKS KINOKUNIYA
YOU CAN DO TAX FREE AT KINOKUNIYA.
お会計 CASHIER
免税 TAX FREE

紀伊國屋書店
KINOKUNIYA ALSO HAS A BRANCH ON THE 6TH FLOOR OF THE TAKASHIMAYA TIMES SQUARE SOUTH BUILDING THAT SELLS FOREIGN-LANGUAGE BOOKS.

IF YOU READ JAPANESE AND DON'T CARE ABOUT TAX FREE, THEN YOU SHOULD VISIT JUNKUDO IN IKEBUKURO, TOKYO'S LARGEST BOOKSTORE.
JUNKUDO
JUNKUDO
THEY HAVE 10 FLOORS PACKED FULL OF JAPANESE BOOKS!

I HOPE YOU ENJOYED MY RECOMMENDATIONS AND FIND BOOKS THAT YOU LIKE!
HAPPY READING!

ART MATERIALS

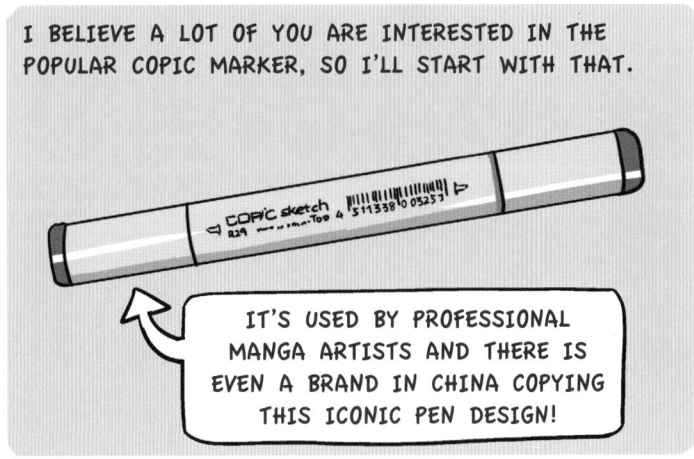

THE SMALLER BUILDING BEHIND IS CALLED K. ITOYA AND SELLS ALL KINDS OF ART MATERIALS.
INCLUDING COPIC MARKERS!

IT HAS A GREAT STATIONERY SECTION TOO, SO IT'S A GOOD PLACE TO DO SOME TAX-FREE SHOPPING.

TOKYU HANDS (SEE PAGE 110) ALSO SELLS A LARGE SELECTION OF ART MATERIALS AT THEIR BIGGER BRANCHES.
COPIC

THE GOOD THING ABOUT SHOPPING HERE IS THAT YOU CAN BUY OTHER PRODUCTS LIKE SKINCARE AND SOUVENIRS, AS WELL AS COPIC MARKERS AND ART MATERIALS TO HIT THE MINIMUM TAX-FREE AMOUNT.

LAST BUT NOT LEAST, THERE'S SEKAIDO'S FLAGSHIP STORE IN SHINJUKU.
ALTHOUGH IT'S NOT TAX FREE, IT OFFERS MANY ART MATERIALS AT 20% BELOW MARKET PRICE (sekaido.co.jp).
SEKAIDO

UNFORTUNATELY, THEY DON'T CARRY THE POPULAR COPIC MARKERS...
BUT WITH 5 FLOORS OF ART MATERIALS, I'M SURE YOU'LL FIND SOMETHING THAT YOU LIKE!

ACKNOWLEDGMENTS & DEDICATION

I WOULD LIKE TO THANK MY JAPANESE FRIENDS WHO ARE ALWAYS HELPFUL ANSWERING MY QUESTIONS AND TREATING ME TO DELICIOUS JAPANESE FOOD WHENEVER I VISIT TOKYO: HIROFUMI MATSUMURA, NAOYA MATSUURA, TOMOYUKI ASHIZAWA AND YUKO HOKAMA. ALSO SPECIAL THANKS TO WAHYU GURUH WIDJAJA FOR ALWAYS HELPING ME BUY GHIBLI TICKETS AND BOOK MY FAVORITE YAKITORI RESTAURANT. I WOULD ALSO LIKE TO THANK MY ASSISTANTS: EMMANUEL HONG AND TAN WEI LIN FOR HELPING ME BLOCK OUT THE BASIC COLORS SO THIS BOOK COULD BE COMPLETED ON TIME.

THIS BOOK IS DEDICATED TO ALL MY FRIENDS AND FANS WHO HAVE BEEN SUPPORTING ME FOR THE PAST 10 YEARS, PARTICULARLY TO MY PATRONS AT www.patreon.com/evacomics

THEY ARE: ALEXY ISKHAKOV, IRENE WONG, JOYCE CHEE, ZENUS, STEFFI LIEW, ALI, COLIN CHIN, KAILIN HUANG, DENVER LU, CAROLINE TSOI, C. LIM, MIHO IWAGUCHI, LEONARD TAN, WM, MIDORI KAME, YUKI TANI, NICHOLAS HONG, JOYCE YAP, NORMAN LEE, CATHERINE TAN, ALEX KWEE, GEORGE RIVERA, AKIHIRO KIKUCHI, LUM SUN YING, MIKE SHAO JIE, EDWIN, LOKE WAI LIAM, QIANYING, ALVIN KOH, TAN CHIN HUI, KOPINUT LO, JEROME LEE, LIN XIANGJUN, REVENTON ARCH, KURONE SHIZUHI, AW MEI QI, JON KHOO, VERENA SEIFERT, CANDY HO, TEOH YI CHIE, JERRY MKP, DIDI AMZAR, VICTOR HENG, JASON LAW, AIZUDDIEN YAKIB, ATSOMNAMBULIST, WILLIAM, CHRISTY WULAN KAMBEY, JONATHAN KHO, TRI CHU, SIOWFEN LOU, KK, BOB QUEK, THOMAS SCHENKER, JAROSPONG SUVARNASUDDHI, YINGYU WANG, DAPHENE LXJ, MISSY LEE, BROOK WEST, GUM ANG, SHAUL HEYMANS, QIAO WEN, SOPHIA ONG, IRFAN YANG, MELISSA CANDRASAPUTRA AND SILVER CHIA.

LASTLY, THANK YOU TO ALL THE READERS AND FANS WHO BOUGHT THIS BOOK!

Published by Tuttle Publishing, an imprint of
Periplus Editions (HK) Ltd

www.tuttlepublishing.com

Copyright © 2019 Evangeline Neo

All rights reserved. No part of this publication may be reproduced or utilized in any form or by any means, electronic or mechanical, including photocopying, recording, or by any information storage and retrieval system, without prior written permission from the publisher.

Library of Congress Control Number: 2018968254

ISBN 978-4-8053-1547-7

Distributed by:
North America, Latin America & Europe
Tuttle Publishing
364 Innovation Drive, North Clarendon
VT 05759-9436 U.S.A.
Tel: 1 (802) 773-8930; Fax: 1 (802) 773-6993
info@tuttlepublishing.com; www.tuttlepublishing.com

Japan
Tuttle Publishing
Yaekari Building 3rd Floor
5-4-12 Osaki Shinagawa-ku, Tokyo 141 0032
Tel: (81) 3 5437-0171; Fax: (81) 3 5437-0755
sales@tuttle.co.jp; www.tuttle.co.jp

Asia Pacific
Berkeley Books Pte. Ltd.
3 Kallang Sector, #04-01, Singapore 349278
Tel: (65) 6741-2178; Fax: (65) 6741-2179
inquiries@periplus.com.sg; www.tuttlepublishing.com

Printed in China 2112EP
24 23 22 21 10 9 8 7 6 5 4 3

TUTTLE PUBLISHING® is a registered trademark of Tuttle Publishing, a division of Periplus Editions (HK) Ltd.

"Books to Span the East and West"

Tuttle Publishing was founded in 1832 in the small New England town of Rutland, Vermont (USA). Our core values remain as strong today as they were then—to publish best-in-class books which bring people together one page at a time. In 1948, we established a publishing office in Japan—and Tuttle is now a leader in publishing English-language books about the arts, languages and cultures of Asia. The world has become a much smaller place today and Asia's economic and cultural influence has grown. Yet the need for meaningful dialogue and information about this diverse region has never been greater. Over the past seven decades, Tuttle has published thousands of books on subjects ranging from martial arts and paper crafts to language learning and literature—and our talented authors, illustrators, designers and photographers have won many prestigious awards. We welcome you to explore the wealth of information available on Asia at www.tuttlepublishing.com.